UNIT 1: COURSE OVERVIEW

This page intentionally left blank

Course Objectives

At the end of this course, the participants should be familiar with:

- ICS applications.
- ICS organizational principles and elements.
- ICS positions and responsibilities.
- ICS facilities and functions.
- ICS planning.

Scope

- Course Introduction
- Course Goals and Objectives
- Introductions and Expectations
- Course Structure and Logistics
- Course Completion

Methodology

The instructors will welcome the students to the course and introduce themselves, providing a brief statement of their backgrounds and experience with the Incident Command System. Next, the students will introduce themselves, providing their names, agencies, and experience with resource management. They will also share their expectations of this course.

The instructors will explain their expectations of the students and provide the students with course administrative information. They will also present the criteria for successful course completion.

Materials

- PowerPoint visuals 1.1 – 1.9
- Instructor Guide
- PowerPoint slides and a computer display system
- Student Manual

Time Plan

A suggested time plan for this unit is shown below. More or less time may be required, based on the experience level of the group.

Topic	Time
Course Introduction	5 minutes
Introductions and Expectations	20 minutes
Course Structure and Logistics	5 minutes
Successful Course Completion	5 minutes
Total Time	**35 minutes**

Course Introduction

Visual 1.1

Instructor Notes: Present the following key points

Welcome the participants to the course.

This course will introduce them to the Incident Command System (ICS). Introduce yourself by providing:

- Your name and organization.
- A brief statement of your experience with emergency or incident response using ICS, and your experience with incidents.

Course Goals and Objectives

Visual 1.2

Instructor Notes: Present the following key points

The goals for this course are for you to:

- Demonstrate basic knowledge of the Incident Command System (ICS).
- Be prepared to coordinate with response partners from all levels of government and the private sector.

This course is designed to provide overall incident management skills rather than tactical expertise. Additional courses are available on developing and implementing incident tactics.

Visual 1.3

Overall Course Objectives

After completion of this course, you should be familiar with ICS:

- Applications.
- Organizational principles and elements.
- Positions and responsibilities.
- Facilities and functions.
- Planning.

FEMA

Visual 1.3
Course Overview

Instructor Notes: Present the following key points

At the completion of the course, you should be familiar with:

- ICS applications.
- ICS organizational principles and elements.
- ICS positions and responsibilities.
- ICS facilities and functions.
- ICS planning.

Introductions and Expectations

Visual 1.4

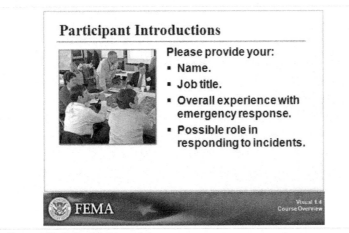

Instructor Notes: Present the following key points

Ask the participants to introduce themselves by providing:

- Their name.
- Their job title.
- A brief statement of their overall experience with emergency or incident response.
- Their possible roles in responding to incidents.

Instructor Note: Some participants may not know what their roles would be during an incident. Explain that this may be a simple as following instructions.

Visual 1.5

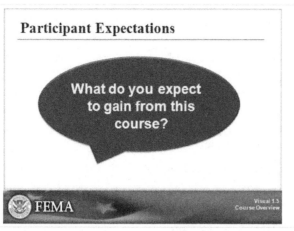

Instructor Notes: Present the following key points

Ask the participants: What do you expect to gain from this course?

Allow the group time to respond. Record their responses on chart paper.

If possible, hang the list of their responses in the training room. Revisit the list at the end of the course to ensure that participants have met their learning objectives

Visual 1.6

Instructor Expectations

- Cooperate with the group.
- Be open minded to new ideas.
- Participate actively in all of the training activities and exercises.
- Return to class at the stated time.
- Use what you learn in the course to perform effectively within an ICS organization.

FEMA

Visual 1.6
Course Overview

Instructor Notes: Present the following key points

Like the participants, you, as the instructor, also have expectations for the course. You expect that everyone will:

- Cooperate with the group.
- Be open minded to new ideas.
- Participate actively in all of the training activities and exercises.
- Return to class at the stated time.
- Use what they learn in the course to perform effectively within an ICS organization.

Course Structure

Visual 1.7

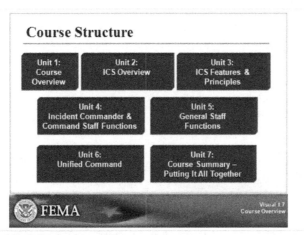

Instructor Notes: Present the following key points

The course is divided into the following seven units:

- Unit 1: Course Overview
- Unit 2: ICS Overview
- Unit 3: ICS Features and Principles
- Unit 4: Incident Commander and Command Staff Functions
- Unit 5: General Staff Functions
- Unit 6: Unified Command
- Unit 7: Course Summary – Putting It All Together

Course Logistics

Visual 1.8

Instructor Notes: Present the following key points

Review the following information:

- Course agenda
- Sign-in sheet
- Review the following housekeeping issues:
- Breaks
- Message and telephone location
- Cell phone policy
- Facilities
- Other concerns

Instructor Note: The course glossary is located at the end of this unit, and they should use it throughout the course. Some of the terms in the glossary may be used differently in ICS than in day-to-day operations (e.g., facilities).

Course Completion

Visual 1.9

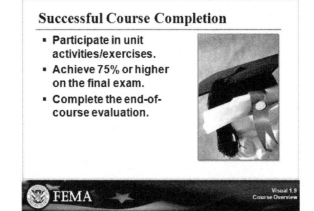

Instructor Notes: Present the following key points

In order to successfully complete this course, you must:

- Participate in unit activities/exercises.
- Achieve 75% or higher on the final exam.
- Complete the end-of-course evaluation.

Ask if anyone has any questions about anything covered in this unit.

The next unit will provide an overview of ICS. Refer to the glossary located at the end of this unit throughout the training session.

DAY 1

- Unit 1: Course Overview (35 minutes)
- Unit 2: ICS Overview (1 hour)
- Unit 3: ICS Features and Principles (2 hours 20 minutes)

- Unit 4: Incident Commander and Command Staff Functions (55 minutes)
- Unit 5: General Staff Functions (2 hours 5 minutes)
- Unit 6: Unified Command (1 hour 5 minutes)
- Unit 7: Course Summary – Putting It All Together (1 hour 30 minutes)

UNIT 2: ICS OVERVIEW

This page intentionally left blank

Unit Objectives

At the end of this unit, the participants should be able to:

- Identify three purposes of the Incident Command System (ICS).
- Identify requirements to use ICS.

Scope

- Unit Introduction
- ICS Overview
- Activity: ICS and Planned Events
- National Preparedness and ICS Requirements
- ICS Benefits
- Activity: Management Challenges
- Unit Summary

Methodology

The instructors will introduce the unit by displaying a visual that outlines the unit objectives.After this introduction to ICS, the instructors will lead a discussion about when participants have used ICS in the past and when they might use it in the future.

The instructors will show a video presentation that explains the benefits of ICS in promoting response partnerships. After the video, the instructors will summarize the key points of the video. To ensure comprehension, the participants will take part in an activity about using ICS for planned events.

The instructors will introduce the group to the importance of the National Incident Management System (NIMS) and its impact on ICS.

The participants will then break into small groups to participate in a scenario-based activity in which they explore how ICS can help to address incident management challenges.

After answering any questions that the participants have, the instructors will summarize the key points from the unit and transition to Unit 3.

Materials

- PowerPoint visuals 2.1 – 2.15
- Instructor Guide
- PowerPoint slides and a computer display system
- Student Manual

Time Plan

A suggested time plan for this unit is shown below. More or less time may be required, based on the experience level of the group.

Topic	Time
Unit Introduction	5 minutes
ICS Overview/Activity: ICS and Planned Events	15 minutes
National Preparedness and ICS Requirements	10 minutes
ICS Benefits	10 minutes
Activity: Management Challenges	15 minutes
Unit Summary	5 minutes
Total Time	**1 hour**

Unit Introduction

Visual 2.1

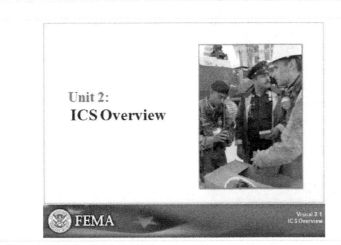

Instructor Notes: Present the following key points

Unit 2 provides a general overview of the Incident Command System, or ICS. The next visual will outline the objectives for this unit.

Visual 2.2

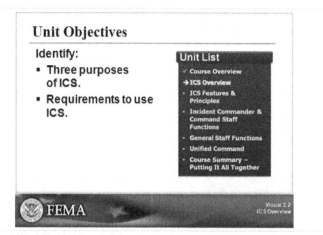

Instructor Notes: Present the following key points

By the end of this unit, you should be able to:

- Identify three purposes of the Incident Command System (ICS).
- Identify requirements to use ICS.
    - National Incident Management System (NIMS)
    - Superfund Amendments and Reauthorization Act (SARA) – 1986
    - Occupational Safety and Health Administration (OSHA) Rule 1910.120
    - State and local regulations

Visual 2.3

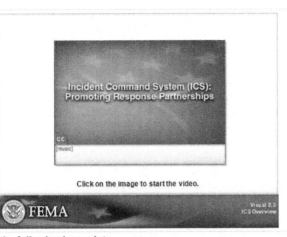

Click on the image to start the video.

Instructor Notes: Present the following key points

The following video summarizes the purposes of ICS.

Video Transcript:

Disaster can strike anytime, anywhere. It takes many forms—a hurricane, an earthquake, a tornado, a flood, a fire or a hazardous spill, or an act of terrorism. An incident can build over days or weeks, or hit suddenly, without warning.

A poorly managed incident response can undermine our safety and well being. With so much at stake, we must effectively manage our response efforts.

Although most incidents are handled locally, partnerships among local, tribal, State, and Federal agencies as well as nongovernmental and private-sector organizations may be required.

As partners, we must respond together in a seamless, coordinated fashion.

The Incident Command System, or ICS, helps ensure integration of our response efforts. ICS is a standardized, on-scene, all-hazards approach to incident management. ICS allows all responders to adopt an integrated organizational structure that matches the complexities and demands of the incident while respecting agency and jurisdictional authorities. Although ICS promotes standardization, it is not without needed flexibility. For example, the ICS organizational structure can expand or contract to meet incident needs.

In this course, you'll learn ICS principles. And more importantly, you'll learn to interface better with your response partners.

ICS Overview

Visual 2.4

> ## What Is ICS?
>
> **ICS:**
>
> - Is a standardized, on-scene, all-hazards incident management concept.
> - Enables a coordinated response among various jurisdictions and agencies.
> - Establishes common processes for planning and management of resources.
> - Allows for integration within a common organizational structure.
>
> **FEMA**
>
> Visual 2.4
> ICS Overview

Instructor Notes: Present the following key points

ICS:

- Is a standardized, on-scene, all-hazards incident management concept.
- Enables a coordinated response among various jurisdictions and agencies.
- Establishes common processes for planning and managing resources.
- Allows for the integration of facilities, equipment, personnel, procedures, and communications operating within a common organizational structure.
- ICS was developed in the 1970s following a series of catastrophic fires in California. Property damage ran into the millions, and many people died or were injured.

The personnel assigned to determine the causes of these disasters studied the case histories and discovered that response problems could rarely be attributed to lack of resources or failure of tactics.

Visual 2.5

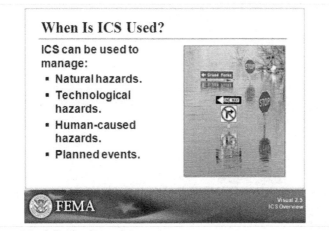

Instructor Notes: Present the following key points

ICS can be used to manage:

- Natural hazards.
- Technological hazards.
- Human-caused hazards.
- Planned events.

Visual 2.6

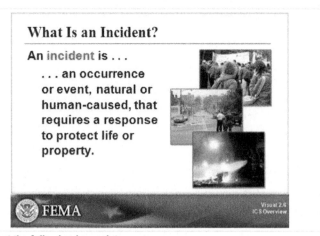

Instructor Notes: Present the following key points

An incident is an occurrence or event, natural or human-caused that requires a response to protect life or property.

Visual 2.7

Activity: ICS & Planned Events

Instructions: Working as a team . . .

1. Briefly describe one example where ICS could be used to manage a planned event (e.g., sporting event).

2. Identify the benefits of using ICS for the selected event.

3. Select a spokesperson. Be prepared to present your example in 5 minutes.

FEMA

Visual 2.7
ICS Overview

Instructor Notes: Present the following key points

Activity Purpose: To illustrate how ICS can be used to address incident management issues, using planned events as an example.

Instructions: Follow the steps below to conduct this activity:

1. Assign the participants to teams.
2. Ask them to work with their teams to develop a brief description of one example where ICS could be used to manage planned events. Participants should also identify the benefits of using ICS for the selected event.
3. Tell the groups to write their examples on chart paper.
4. Ask the participants in each group to select a spokesperson to present the group's response.
5. Tell the groups that they will have 5 minutes to complete this activity.

Time: 5 minutes

Debrief Instructions:

1. Monitor the time. Notify the participants when 2 minutes remain.
2. Have each spokesperson present their group's answers.
3. Point out the importance of practicing ICS in planned events.
4. If not mentioned by the groups, emphasize the importance of including outside response agencies in the ICS organization for planned events.

National Preparedness and ICS Requirements

Visual 2.8

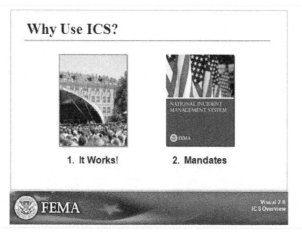

Instructor Notes: Present the following key points

Review the following points about the value of using ICS:

- ICS works! It saves lives! Life safety is the top priority for ICS response.
- The use of ICS is mandated by the National Incident Management System (NIMS). NIMS provides a systematic, proactive approach guiding departments and agencies at all levels of government, the private sector, and nongovernmental organizations to work seamlessly to prepare for, prevent, respond to, recover from, and mitigate the effects of incidents, regardless of cause, size, location, or complexity, in order to reduce the loss of life and property, and harm to the environment.

In addition to the NIMS mandate, the following laws require the use of ICS:

- The Superfund Amendments and Reauthorization Act (SARA) of 1986 established Federal regulations for handling hazardous materials. SARA directed the Occupational Safety and Health Administration (OSHA) to establish rules for operations at hazardous materials incidents.
- OSHA rule 1910.120, effective March 6, 1990, requires all organizations that handle hazardous materials to use ICS. The regulation states: "The Incident Command System shall be established by those employers for the incidents that will be under their control and shall interface with other organizations or agencies who may respond to such an incident."

Note that the Environmental Protection Agency (EPA) requires States to use ICS at hazardous materials incidents.

According to the National Integration Center, "institutionalizing the use of ICS" means that government officials, incident managers, and emergency response organizations at all jurisdictional levels must adopt ICS. Actions to institutionalize the use of ICS take place at two levels:

- Policy Level: At the policy level, institutionalizing ICS means government officials (i.e., Governors, mayors, county and city managers, tribal leaders, and others) must:
    - Adopt ICS through executive order, proclamation, or legislation as the jurisdiction's official incident response system; and
    - Direct that incident managers and response organizations in their jurisdictions train, exercise, and use ICS in their response operations.
- Organizational Level: At the organizational/operational level, evidence that incident managers and emergency response organizations are institutionalizing ICS would include the following:
    - ICS is being integrated into functional and system-wide emergency operations policies, plans, and procedures.
    - ICS training is planned or underway for responders, supervisors, and command-level officers.
    - Responders at all levels are participating in and/or coordinating ICS-oriented exercises that involve responders from multiple disciplines and jurisdictions.

Visual 2.9

National Incident Management System (NIMS)

What ? . . . NIMS provides a consistent nationwide template . . .

Who? . . . to enable Federal, State, tribal, and local governments, the private sector, and nongovernmental organizations to work together . . .

How? . . . to prepare for, prevent, respond to, recover from, and mitigate the effects of incidents regardless of cause, size, location, or complexity . . .

Why? . . . in order to reduce the loss of life and property, and harm to the environment.

FEMA

Visual 2.9
ICS Overview

Instructor Notes: Present the following key points

The National Incident Management System provides a consistent framework for incident management at all jurisdictional levels regardless of the cause, size, or complexity of the incident. NIMS is not an operational incident management or resource allocation plan.

Visual 2.10

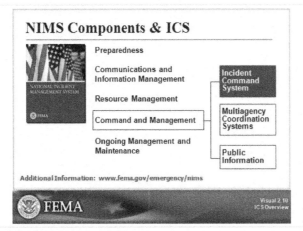

Instructor Notes: Present the following key points

NIMS represents a core set of doctrine, concepts, principles, terminology, and organizational processes that enables effective, efficient, and collaborative incident management.

- Preparedness: Effective emergency management and incident response activities begin with a host of preparedness activities conducted on an ongoing basis, in advance of any potential incident. Preparedness involves an integrated combination of planning, procedures and protocols, training and exercises, personnel qualifications and certification, and equipment certification.
- Communications and Information Management: Emergency management and incident response activities rely upon communications and information systems that provide a common operating picture to all command and coordination sites. NIMS describes the requirements necessary for a standardized framework for communications and emphasizes the need for a common operating picture. NIMS is based upon the concepts of interoperability, reliability, scalability, portability, and the resiliency and redundancy of communications and information systems.
- Resource Management: Resources (such as personnel, equipment, and/or supplies) are needed to support critical incident objectives. The flow of resources must be fluid and adaptable to the requirements of the incident. NIMS defines standardized mechanisms and establishes the resource management process to identify requirements, order and acquire, mobilize, track and report, recover and demobilize, reimburse, and inventory resources.
- Command and Management: The Command and Management component within NIMS is designed to enable effective and efficient incident management and coordination by providing flexible, standardized incident management structures. The structures are based on three key organizational constructs: the Incident Command System, Multiagency Coordination Systems, and Public Information.
- Ongoing Management and Maintenance: Within the auspices of Ongoing Management and Maintenance, there are two components: The National Integration Center (NIC) and Supporting Technologies.

Discussion Questions

Visual 2.11

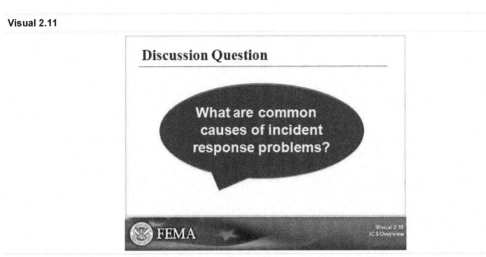

Instructor Notes: Present the following key points

Ask the participants: What are some common causes of incident response problems?

Acknowledge the participants' responses. If not mentioned by the group, include the following:

- After-action reports from ineffective incident responses find that response problems are far more likely to result from inadequate management than from any other single cause.

The following page further explains causes of weaknesses in incident management.

ICS Benefits

Visual 2.12

Instructor Notes: Present the following key points

Without ICS, incident responses typically result in:

- Lack of accountability, including unclear chains of command and supervision.
- Poor communication, due to both inefficient uses of available communications systems and conflicting codes and terminology.
- Lack of an orderly, systematic planning process.
- No common, flexible, predesigned management structure that enabled commanders to delegate responsibilities and manage workloads efficiently.
- No predefined methods to integrate interagency requirements into the management structure and planning process effectively.

Using ICS enables us to avoid these weaknesses in all types of incident responses.

Visual 2.13

Instructor Notes: Present the following key points

By using management best practices, ICS helps to ensure:

- The safety of responders, faculty, workers, and others.
- The achievement of response objectives.
- The efficient use of resources.

Visual 2.14

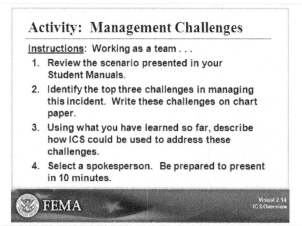

Instructor Notes: Present the following key points

Activity Purpose: The purpose of this activity is to demonstrate the benefits of ICS.

Instructions: Follow the steps below to conduct this activity:

1. Assign the participants to groups of five or six.
2. Tell the participants to work as a team to review the scenario presented on the next page in their Student Manuals.
3. Explain that each group should identify the top three challenges for officials to manage this incident. Each group should write the challenges on chart paper. The groups should also discuss how ICS could be used to address these challenges.
4. Ask the participants in each group to select a spokesperson.
5. Inform the group that they will have 10 minutes to complete this activity.

Time: 10 minutes

Debrief Instructions:

1. Monitor the time. Notify the participants when 5 minutes remain.
2. Have each spokesperson present their group's answers.

Scenario: Continuing severe weather is causing widespread damage. 9-1-1 operators are receiving conflicting reports about life-safety needs, including a possible structural collapse of an assisted living facility.

Discussion Questions:

1. What are the priorities?
2. What are the incident management challenges? (Think about how ICS may address these challenges!)
3. Who needs to be involved?

There is no one correct answer, but if not mentioned by participants, note that using management best practices, ICS helps to ensure:

- The safety of responders and others.
- The achievement of tactical objectives.
- efficient use of resources.

Unit Summary

Visual 2.15

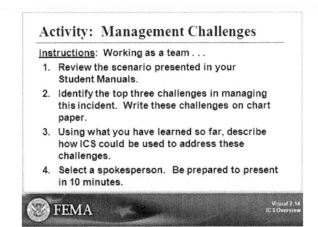

Instructor Notes: Present the following key points

ICS:

- Is a standardized management tool for meeting the demands of small or large emergency and non-emergency situations.
- Represents best practices, and has become the standard for emergency management across the country.
- May be used for planned events, natural disasters, and acts of terrorism.
- Is a key feature of NIMS.

Ask if anyone has any questions about anything covered in this unit.

The next unit will cover the basic features of ICS.

32

UNIT 3: ICS FEATURES AND PRINCIPLES

This page intentionally left blank

Unit Objectives

At the end of this unit, the participants should be able to:

- Describe the basic features of ICS.
- Select the correct terminology for ICS facilities.
- Identify common tasks related to personal accountability.

Scope

- Unit Introduction
- ICS Features
- Standardization
- Command
- Planning and Organization Structure
- Facilities and Resources
- Communications and Information Management
- Professionalism
- Unit Summary

Methodology

The instructors will begin by explaining that this unit provides an overview of the basic features and principles of the Incident Command System, or ICS. Instructors will display a visual that outlines the unit objectives.

After reviewing the unit objectives, the instructors will provide information on ICS features and principles, first by showing a video. Next, they will explain the importance of standardization by using common terminology and plain English during an incident response.

Next, the instructors will introduce establishment and transfer of command. They will define command and then describe the process for transferring command, or moving responsibility for incident command from one Incident Commander to another. The instructors will provide examples of situations where a transfer of command would be needed. They will ask participants to identify topics to include in a transfer of command briefing. The instructors will cover the concepts of chain of command and unity of command. The group will consider a scenario to segue into discussion of incident objectives, and the priorities followed in addressing objectives in an incident.

Next, the instructors will explain the differences between ICS organizational structure and day- to-day administrative organizational structure. The instructors will cover how objectives are established to manage the incident. They will describe the ICS flexible modular organization, including the fact that only functions or positions that are necessary will be filled.

The next ICS feature covered is the development of an Incident Action Plan, or IAP. The instructors will identify the four elements that every IAP must contain. The participants will then work in teams to identify four items to include in an IAP for the incident used in Unit 2.

The instructors will explain the importance of maintaining a manageable span of control: Per ICS guidelines, a supervisor optimally should not have more than five subordinates. The instructor will ask the participants what types of incidents warrant a low span-of-control ratio. Students will consider an incident scenario, and determine whether the span of control is sufficient.

Next the group will view a video that presents a "virtual tour" of standard ICS facilities. The instructors will then briefly review predesignated incident facilities. The next ICS feature covered is resource management. Resources include personnel as well as equipment.

The instructors will then explain the importance of developing an integrated voice and data communications system, and ensuring that communications systems among various responders are interoperable. The instructors will lead a discussion of the importance of information and intelligence management. They will use an activity to ask the group for examples of information and intelligence that could be used to manage an incident.

The instructors will then explain the importance of professionalism, which includes applying principles of accountability and carrying out responsibilities involved in dispatch and deployment. The group will discuss complications that arise from self-deployment, and consider problems created by self-deployment in an emergency scenario.

At the end of the unit, the participants will answer questions about the ICS features covered.

The instructors will then summarize the key ICS features and principles, and transition to Unit 4.

Materials

- PowerPoint visuals 3.1 – 3.44
- Instructor Guide
- PowerPoint slides and a computer display system
- Student Manual

Time Plan

A suggested time plan for this unit is shown below. More or less time may be required, based on the experience level of the group.

Topic	Time
Unit Introduction	5 minutes

Topic	Time
ICS Features	10 minutes
Standardization	5 minutes
Command	12 minutes
Activity: Assuming Command	10 minutes
Planning and Organizational Structure	8 minutes
Activity: Incident Action Plan	10 minutes
Activity: Span of Control	10 minutes
Facilities and Resources	15 minutes
Activity: Staging Areas	10 minutes
Communications and Information Management	10 minutes
Activity: Information Management	10 minutes
Professionalism	10 minutes
Activity: Deployment	10 minutes
Unit Summary	5 minutes
Total Time	**2 hours, 20 minutes**

Unit Introduction

Visual 3.1

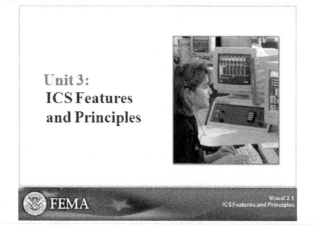

Instructor Notes: Present the following key points

This unit will provide an overview of the basic features and principles of the Incident Command System (ICS):

- ICS management principles
- ICS core system features

Visual 3.2

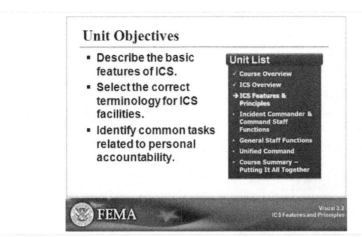

Instructor Notes: Present the following key points

By the end of this unit you should be able to:

- Describe the basic features of ICS.
- Select the correct terminology for ICS facilities.
- Identify common tasks related to personal accountability.

ICS Features

Visual 3.3

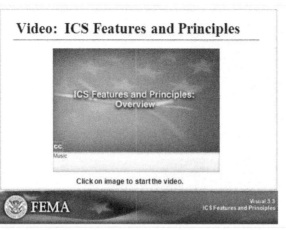

Instructor Notes: Present the following key points

The following video will introduce this lesson on ICS features and principles. The lesson covers each of these ICS features in detail.

Video Transcript:

[Narrator]

As you learned in the previous lesson, ICS is based on proven management principles, which contribute to the strength and efficiency of the overall system.

ICS incorporates a wide range of management features and principles, beginning with the use of common terminology and clear text.

[David Burns, Emergency Preparedness Manager, University of California Los Angeles] Communication is probably one of the most essential elements of ICS. It's important that we know how to communicate.

[Daryl Lee Spiewak, Emergency Programs Manager, the Brazos River Authority]

If the terms that I use mean different things to different people, we're going to have a hard time communicating and doing what needs to be done to accomplish our mission.

[Narrator]

ICS emphasizes effective planning, including management by objectives and reliance on an Incident Action Plan.

[Roberta Runge, EPA National NIMS Coordinator]

You have to coordinate on what your end objective is. All up and down the chain, you have to have a common end goal. So you can establish your objectives, you can ensure they're in the Incident Action Plan, and you can ensure that they are in agreement with the other Incident Action Plans that are produced by agencies.

[Narrator]

The ICS features related to command structure include chain of command and unity of command.

[Bill Campbell, Director of Training, New York State Emergency Management Office] One of the benefits is it gets all of the different organizations working under the same framework.

[Narrator]

ICS helps ensure full utilization of all incident resources by:

- Maintaining a manageable span of control,
- Establishing predesignated incident locations and facilities,
- Implementing resource management practices, and
- Ensuring integrated communications.

ICS supports responders and decision makers through effective information and intelligence management and helps establish a common operating picture.

[Kristy Plourde, NIMS Program Coordinator, U.S. Coast Guard]

The common operating picture is a critical thing that the Coast Guard has been working hard on recently for ourselves because it's something that helps us maintain a better operational picture and it's more consistent across the board—everyone up and down the chain of command and across to other agencies understand the same picture.

[Narrator]

ICS counts on each of us taking personal accountability for our own actions. And finally, the mobilization process helps ensure that incident objectives can be achieved while responders remain safe.

[Kristy Plourde, NIMS Program Coordinator, U.S. Coast Guard] To have NIMS work effectively, it's got to be top-down support.

[Narrator]

The ICS features covered in this lesson form the basis for effective, team-based incident response at all levels.

Visual 3.4

Instructor Notes: Present the following key points

Review the features presented on the visual. Refer to the next two pages in your Student Manual, which provide more detail about each feature.

The essential ICS features are listed below:

Standardization:

- Common Terminology: Using common terminology helps to define organizational functions, incident facilities, resource descriptions, and position titles.

Command:

- Establishment and Transfer of Command: The command function must be clearly established from the beginning of an incident. When command is transferred, the process must include a briefing that captures all essential information for continuing safe and effective operations.
- Chain of Command and Unity of Command: Chain of command refers to the orderly line of authority within the ranks of the incident management organization. Unity of command means that every individual has a designated supervisor to whom he or she reports at the scene of the incident. These principles clarify reporting relationships and eliminate the confusion caused by multiple, conflicting directives. Incident managers at all levels must be able to control the actions of all personnel under their supervision.

Planning/Organizational Structure:

- Management by Objectives: Includes establishing overarching objectives; developing and issuing assignments, plans, procedures, and protocols; establishing specific, measurable objectives for various incident management functional activities; and directing efforts to attain the established objectives.
- Modular Organization: The Incident Command organizational structure develops in a top-down, modular fashion that is based on the size and complexity of the incident, as well as the specifics of the hazard environment created by the incident.
- Incident Action Planning: Incident Action Plans (IAPs) provide a coherent means of communicating the overall incident objectives in the contexts of both operational and support activities.
- Manageable Span of Control: Span of control is key to effective and efficient incident management. Within ICS, the span of control of any individual with incident management supervisory responsibility should range from three to seven subordinates.

Facilities and Resources:

- Incident Locations and Facilities: Various types of operational locations and support facilities are established in the vicinity of an incident to accomplish a variety of purposes. Typical predesignated facilities include Incident Command Posts, Bases, Camps, Staging Areas, Mass Casualty Triage Areas, and others as required.
- Comprehensive Resource Management: Resource management includes processes for categorizing, ordering, dispatching, tracking, and recovering resources. It also includes processes for reimbursement for resources, as appropriate. Resources are defined as personnel, teams, equipment, supplies, and facilities available or potentially available for assignment or allocation in support of incident management and emergency response activities.

Communications/Information Management:

- Integrated Communications: Incident communications are facilitated through the development and use of a common communications plan and interoperable communications processes and architectures.
- Information and Intelligence Management: The incident management organization must establish a process for gathering, sharing, and managing incident-related information and intelligence.

Professionalism:

- Accountability: Effective accountability at all jurisdictional levels and within individual functional areas during incident operations is essential. To that end, the following principles must be adhered to:

- Check-In: All responders, regardless of agency affiliation, must report in to receive an assignment in accordance with the procedures established by the Incident Commander.
- Incident Action Plan: Response operations must be directed and coordinated as outlined in the IAP.
- Unity of Command: Each individual involved in incident operations will be assigned to only one supervisor.
- Span of Control: Supervisors must be able to adequately supervise and control their subordinates, as well as communicate with and manage all resources under their supervision.
- Resource Tracking: Supervisors must record and report resource status changes as they occur. (This topic is covered in a later unit.)
- Dispatch/Deployment: Personnel and equipment should respond only when requested or when dispatched by an appropriate authority.

Standardization

Visual 3.5

Common Terminology – No Codes!

Using common terminology helps define:

- Organizational functions.
- Incident facilities.
- Resource descriptions.
- Position titles.

FEMA

Visual 3.5
ICS Features and Principles

Instructor Notes: Present the following key points

The ability to communicate within ICS is absolutely critical. An essential method for ensuring the ability to communicate is by using common terminology and clear text.

A critical part of an effective multiagency incident management system is for all communications to be in plain English. That is, use clear text. Do not use radio codes, departmental codes, or jargon.

Visual 3.6

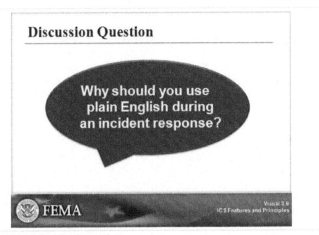

Instructor Notes: Present the following key points

Ask the participants: Even if you use codes on a daily basis, why should you use plain English during an incident response?

Allow the participants time to respond. If not mentioned by the group, tell the participants that it is important to use plain English during an incident response because:

- Often there is more than one organization involved in an incident.
- Ambiguous codes and acronyms have proven to be major obstacles in communications.
- Often organizations have a variety of codes and acronyms that they use routinely during normal operations. When these codes and acronyms are used on an incident, confusion is often the result.
- NIMS requires that all responders use "plain English," referred to as "clear text."

Visual 3.7

Why Plain English?

EMT = Emergency Medical Treatment
EMT = Emergency Medical Technician
EMT = Emergency Management Team
EMT = Eastern Mediterranean Time (GMT+0200)
EMT = Effective Methods Team
EMT = Effects Management Tool
EMT = El Monte, CA (airport code)
EMT = Electron Microscope Tomography
EMT = Email Money Transfer

FEMA

Visual 3.7
ICS Features and Principles

Instructor Notes: Present the following key points

Refer to the following examples of different meanings of a common acronym.

EMT = Emergency Medical Treatment

EMT = Emergency Medical Technician

EMT = Emergency Management Team

EMT = Eastern Mediterranean Time (GMT+0200)

EMT = Effective Methods Team

EMT = Effects Management Tool

EMT = El Monte, CA (airport code)

EMT = Electron Microscope Tomography

EMT = Email Money Transfer

Ask the participants for examples of other codes or jargon that could be misunderstood by responders from different agencies.

Command

Visual 3.7

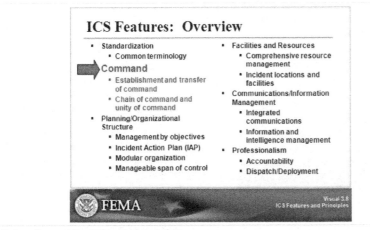

Instructor Notes: Present the following key points

The next part of this unit covers command, including:

- Establishment and transfer of command.
- Chain of command and unity of command.

Visual 3.9

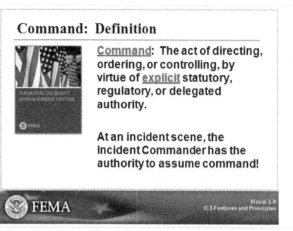

Instructor Notes: Present the following key points

NIMS defines command as the act of directing, ordering, or controlling by virtue of explicit statutory, regulatory, or delegated authority.

At an incident scene, the Incident Commander has the authority to assume command.

The Incident Commander should have the level of training, experience, and expertise to serve in this capacity. It is quite possible that the Incident Commander may not be the highest ranking official on scene.

Visual 3.10

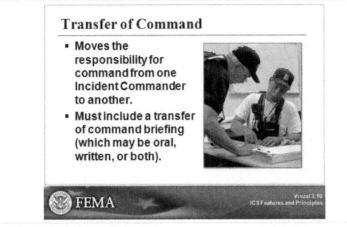

Instructor Notes: Present the following key points

The next ICS feature is transfer of command.

- The process of moving the responsibility for incident command from one Incident Commander to another is called transfer of command.
- The transfer of command process always includes a transfer of command briefing, which may be oral, written, or a combination of both.
- When a transfer of command takes place, it is important to announce the change to the rest of the incident staff.

Visual 3.11

When Command Is Transferred

- A more qualified Incident Commander arrives.
- A jurisdiction or agency is legally required to take command.
- Incident complexity changes.
- The current Incident Commander needs to rest.

Visual 3.11
ICS Features and Principles

Instructor Notes: Present the following key points

There are several possible reasons that command might be transferred. Transfer of command may take place when:

- A more qualified Incident Commander arrives and assumes command.
- A jurisdiction or agency is legally required to take command. For example, the Federal Bureau of Investigation (FBI) is legally required to take the lead for investigations of terrorist incidents.
- The incident changes in complexity. For example, an incident might start in a small area, but spread into the surrounding community, affecting multiple jurisdictions, institutions, or agencies.
- The current Incident Commander needs to rest. On long or extended incidents, there is normally turnover of personnel to accommodate work/rest requirements.

Visual 3.12

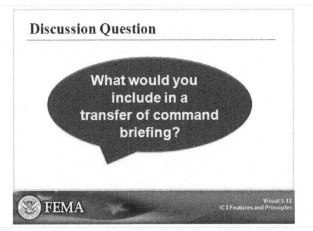

Instructor Notes: Present the following key points

The transfer of command process always includes a thorough transfer of command briefing, which may be oral, written, or a combination of both.

It is also important to remember that the rest of the incident staff should be notified of the transfer of command.

Ask the participants: What would you include in a transfer of command briefing?

Hint: Refer to the additional information on the next page!

The process of moving the responsibility for incident command from one Incident Commander to another is called "transfer of command." It should be recognized that transition of command on an expanding incident is to be expected. It does not reflect on the competency of the current Incident Commander.

There are five important steps in effectively assuming command of an incident in progress.

Step 1: The incoming Incident Commander should, if at all possible, personally perform an assessment of the incident situation with the existing Incident Commander.

Step 2: The incoming Incident Commander must be adequately briefed. This briefing must be by the current Incident Commander, and take place face-to-face if possible. The briefing must cover the following:

- Incident history (what has happened)
- Priorities and objectives
- Current plan
- Resource assignments
- Incident organization
- Resources ordered/needed
- Facilities established
- Status of communications
- Any constraints or limitations
- Incident potential
- Delegation of authority

Step 3: After the incident briefing, the incoming Incident Commander should determine an appropriate time for transfer of command.

Step 4: At the appropriate time, notice of a change in incident command should be made to:

- Agency headquarters.
- General Staff members (if designated).
- Command Staff members (if designated).
- All incident personnel.

Step 5: The incoming Incident Commander may give the previous Incident Commander another assignment on the incident. There are several advantages to this strategy:

- The initial Incident Commander retains first-hand knowledge at the incident site.
- This strategy allows the initial Incident Commander to observe the progress of the incident and to gain experience.

Visual 3.13

> ## Chain of Command
>
> Chain of command:
>
> - Is an orderly line of authority within the response organization.
> - Allows incident managers to direct and control the actions of all personnel under their supervision.
> - Avoids confusion by requiring that orders flow from supervisors.
> - Does not prevent personnel from sharing information.
>
> 🛡️ **FEMA** Visual 3.13
> ICS Features and Principles

Instructor Notes: Present the following key points

Chain of command is an orderly line of authority within the ranks of the incident management organization. Chain of command:

- Allows incident managers to direct and control the actions of all personnel under their supervision.
- Avoids confusion by requiring that orders flow from supervisors.

Chain of command does not prevent personnel from directly communicating with each other to ask for or share information.

The features and principles used to manage an incident differ from day-to-day management approaches. Effective incident management relies on a tight command and control structure. Although information is exchanged freely through the ICS structure, strict adherence must be paid to top-down direction.

To make ICS work, each of us must commit to following this command and control approach.

Visual 3.14

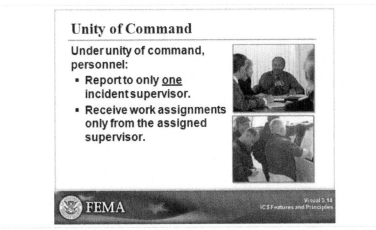

Instructor Notes: Present the following key points

Under unity of command, personnel:

- Report to only one ICS supervisor.
- Receive work assignments only from their ICS supervisors.

Visual 3.15

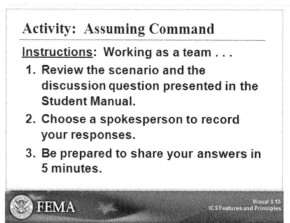

Instructor Notes: Present the following key points

Activity Purpose: To reinforce participants' understanding of what to do when assuming command and transition to a discussion of incident objectives and action planning.

Instructions: Working as a team:

1. Review the scenario and the discussion question presented in the Student Manual.
2. Choose a spokesperson to record your responses.
3. Be prepared to share your answers in 5 minutes.

Time: 10 minutes

Debrief Instructions:

1. Monitor the time. Notify the participants when 2 minutes remain.
2. Have each spokesperson present their group's answers.

Scenario: An unexpected flash flood has struck a small community. Homes, schools, and the business district have been evacuated. Damage to critical infrastructure includes contamination of the water supply, downed power lines, and damaged roads.

Ask the participants: What is the first action you would take?

Acknowledge the groups' responses. If not mentioned by the groups, add that they should:

- Size up the situation.
- Take measures to ensure life safety.

Planning and Organizational Structure

Visual 3.16

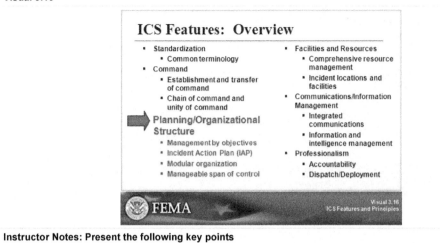

Instructor Notes: Present the following key points

The next part of this unit covers planning and organizational structure, including:

- Management by objectives.
- Incident Action Plan (IAP).
- Modular organization.
- Manageable span of control.

Visual 3.17

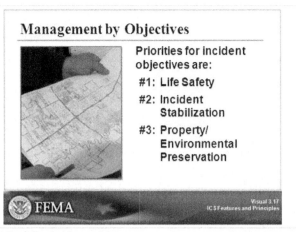

Instructor Notes: Present the following key points

Incident objectives are used to ensure that everyone within the ICS organization has a clear understanding of what needs to be accomplished.

Priorities for incident objectives are:

1. Life safety.
2. Incident stabilization.
3. Property/Environmental preservation.

Visual 3.18

ICS Organization

Differs from day-to-day organizational structures and positions by:

- Using unique ICS position titles and organizational structures.
- Assigning personnel based on expertise, not rank. For example, a director may not hold that title when deployed under an ICS structure.

FEMA

Visual 3.18
ICS Features and Principles

Instructor Notes: Present the following key points

The ICS organization is unique but easy to understand. There is no correlation between the ICS organization and the administrative structure of any single agency or jurisdiction. This is deliberate, because confusion over different position titles and organizational structures has been a significant stumbling block to effective incident management in the past.

For example, someone who serves as a director every day may not hold that title when deployed under an ICS structure.

Visual 3.19

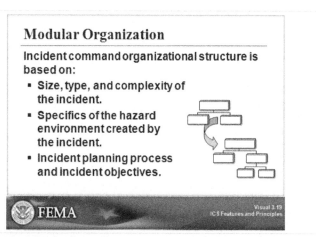

Instructor Notes: Present the following key points

The ICS organizational structure develops in a top-down, modular fashion that is based on the size and complexity of the incident, as well as the specifics of the hazard environment created by the incident. As incident complexity increases, the organization expands from the top down as functional responsibilities are delegated.

The ICS organizational structure is flexible. When needed, separate functional elements can be established and subdivided to enhance internal organizational management and external coordination. As the ICS organizational structure expands, the number of management positions also expands to adequately address the requirements of the incident.

In a later unit, we'll look at how the Operations Section expands and contracts based on span of control.

Visual 3.20

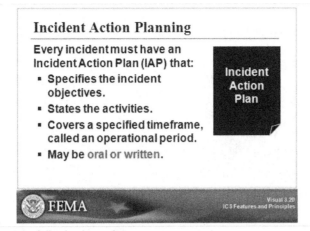

Incident Action Planning

Every incident must have an Incident Action Plan (IAP) that:
- Specifies the incident objectives.
- States the activities.
- Covers a specified timeframe, called an operational period.
- May be oral or written.

FEMA

Visual 3.20
ICS Features and Principles

Instructor Notes: Present the following key points

Every response has a strategy—like a lesson plan—called an Incident Action Plan (IAP). The Incident Commander must ensure that the IAP:

- Specifies the incident objectives.
- States the activities to be completed.
- Covers a specified timeframe, called an operational period.
- May be oral or written—except for hazardous materials incidents, which require a written IAP.

Even the smallest of incidents are managed by incident objectives and plans. The plan can be as simple as the next steps the Incident Commander plans to do. The steps can be orally communicated to the rest of the ICS organization.

Visual 3.21

Elements of an Incident Action Plan

Every IAP must have four elements:

- What do we want to do?
- Who is responsible for doing it?
- How do we communicate with each other?
- What is the procedure if someone is injured?

FEMA

Visual 3.21
ICS Features and Principles

Instructor Notes: Present the following key points

Every IAP must answer the following four questions:

- What do we want to do?
- Who is responsible for doing it?
- How do we communicate with each other?
- What is the procedure if someone is injured?

Visual 3.22

> ## Activity: Incident Action Plan
>
> <u>Instructions</u>: Working as a team . . .
>
> 1. Identify four items you would include in an IAP for the severe weather scenario in Unit 2.
> 2. Write these items on chart paper.
> 3. Select a spokesperson. Be prepared to present in 5 minutes.
>
> FEMA
> Visual 3.22
> ICS Features and Principles

Instructor Notes: Present the following key points

Activity Purpose: To illustrate how to develop an IAP.

Instructions: Working in groups:

1. Identify four items they would include in an Incident Action Plan for the severe weather scenario from Unit 2
2. Record the IAP elements on chart paper.
3. Select a spokesperson to report back to the group. Be prepared to share your answers in 5 minutes.

Time: 10 minutes

Debrief Instructions:

1. Monitor the time. Notify the participants when 2 minutes remain.
2. Have each spokesperson present their group's answers.

Scenario: Continuing severe weather is causing widespread damage. 9-1-1 operators are receiving conflicting reports about life-safety needs, including a possible structural collapse of an assisted living facility.

Ask the participants: What is the first action you would take?

Acknowledge the groups' responses. If not mentioned by the groups, add that they should include:

- What they want to do.
- Who is responsible for doing it.
- How they will communicate with one another.
- What are the risks to responders.
- The procedures if someone is injured.

Visual 3.23

Manageable Span of Control

Span of control:

- Pertains to the number of individuals or resources that one supervisor can manage effectively during an incident.
- Is key to effective and efficient incident management.

Supervisor

Resource 1

Resource 2

Resource 3

FEMA

Visual 3.23
ICS Features and Principles

Instructor Notes: Present the following key points

Another basic ICS feature concerns the supervisory structure of the organization. Maintaining adequate span of control throughout the ICS organization is very important.

Span of control pertains to the number of individuals or resources that one supervisor can manage effectively during an incident.

Maintaining an effective span of control is important at incidents where safety and accountability are a top priority.

Supervisors must be able to adequately supervise and control their subordinates, as well as communicate with and manage all resources under their supervision.

Visual 3.24

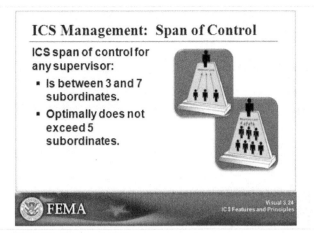

Instructor Notes: Present the following key points

Review the following key points:

- Another basic ICS feature concerns the supervisory structure of the organization.
- Maintaining adequate span of control throughout the ICS organization is very important.
- Span of control pertains to the number of individuals or resources that one supervisor can manage effectively during an incident.
- The type of incident, nature of the task, hazards and safety factors, and distances between personnel and resources all influence span of control considerations. Maintaining an effective span of control is particularly important on incidents where safety and accountability are top priorities.
- Effective span of control on incidents may vary from three to seven, and a ratio of one supervisor to five reporting elements is recommended.

Ask the participants: What types of incidents warrant a low span-of-control ratio?

Example:

Which organization might warrant a lower supervisory span of control (lower ratio of subordinates to each supervisor)?

- Search and Rescue Task Force, or Cost Unit within the Finance/Admin Section

The Search and Rescue Task Force would most likely warrant a lower supervisory span of control. The type of incident, nature of the task, hazards and safety factors, and distances between personnel and resources all influence span of control considerations.

Visual 3.25

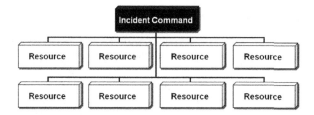

Instructor Notes: Present the following key points

Activity Purpose: To reinforce participants' understanding of span of control.

Instructions: Working individually:

1. Review the scenario and answer the question presented in the Student Manual.
2. Be prepared to share your answer in 5 minutes.

Time: 10 minutes

Instructor Debrief Instructions: Ask for volunteers to present their answers.

Scenario: A water main has broken. Resources are working to repair the break and reroute traffic.

Ask the participants: Is the span of control consistent with ICS guidelines?

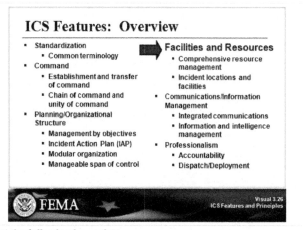

Acknowledge the participants' responses. If not mentioned by the participants, mention that:

- The span of control is NOT consistent with ICS guidelines.
- ICS span of control for any supervisor is between three and seven subordinates and optimally does not exceed five subordinates.

Facilities and Resources

Visual 3.26

ICS Features: Overview

- Standardization
  - Common terminology
- Command
  - Establishment and transfer of command
  - Chain of command and unity of command
- Planning/Organizational Structure
  - Management by objectives
  - Incident Action Plan (IAP)
  - Modular organization
  - Manageable span of control

Facilities and Resources
- Comprehensive resource management
- Incident locations and facilities
- Communications/Information Management
  - Integrated communications
  - Information and intelligence management
- Professionalism
  - Accountability
  - Dispatch/Deployment

FEMA
Visual 3.26
ICS Features and Principles

Instructor Notes: Present the following key points

The next part of this unit covers facilities and resources, including:

- Comprehensive resource management.
- Incident locations and facilities.

Visual 3.27

Instructor Notes: Present the following key points

Review the following key points:

- Incident activities may be accomplished from a variety of operational locations and support facilities.
- The Incident Commander identifies and establishes needed facilities depending on incident needs. Standardized names are used to identify types of facilities.
- In order to integrate with community responders, it is important to be familiar with the standard ICS facilities.

Video Transcript:

This presentation introduces the ICS facilities. In less complex incidents, you most likely will not need many of the standard ICS facilities. However, in large incidents, such as a hurricane or earthquake, it is likely that all of these facilities will be necessary.

The Incident Command Post, or ICP, is the location from which the Incident Commander oversees all incident operations. There should only be one ICP for each incident, but it may change locations during the event. Every incident must have some form of an Incident Command Post. The ICP may be located outside, in a vehicle, trailer, or tent, or within a building. The ICP will be positioned outside of the present and potential hazard zone but close enough to the incident to maintain command.

Staging Areas are temporary locations at an incident where personnel and equipment wait to be assigned. Staging Areas should be located close enough to the incident for a timely response, but far enough away to be out of the immediate impact zone. In large, complex incidents, there may be more than one Staging Area at an incident. Staging Areas can be co-located with other ICS facilities.

A Base is the location from which primary logistics and administrative functions are coordinated and administered.

A Camp is the location where resources may be kept to support incident operations if a Base is not accessible to all resources. Camps are equipped and staffed to provide food, water, sleeping areas, and sanitary services.

A Helibase is the location from which helicopter-centered air operations are conducted. Helibases are generally used on a more long-term basis and include such services as fueling and maintenance.

Helispots are more temporary locations at the incident, where helicopters can safely land and take off. Multiple Helispots may be used.

Let's review the different ICS facilities covered in this video.

- The Incident Command Post is the location from which the Incident Commander oversees all incident operations.
- Staging Areas are where personnel and equipment are gathered while waiting to be assigned.
- A Base is the location from which primary logistics and administrative functions are coordinated and administered.
- A Helibase is the location from which helicopter-centered air operations are conducted.
- Helispots are more temporary locations at the incident, where helicopters can safely land and take off.

Visual 3.28

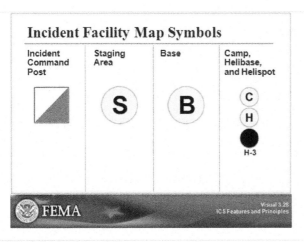

Instructor Notes: Present the following key points

In ICS, it is important to be able to identify the map symbols associated with the basic incident facilities.

The map symbols used to represent each of the six basic ICS facilities are shown in the illustration.

Ask the participants: Helicopters were taking off and landing at a football field after a tornado severely damaged the surrounding area. What map symbol would indicate this ICS facility?

Acknowledge the participants' answers. If not mentioned by the group, explain that the ICS facility could be a Helibase or Helispot and point out the symbols in the visual.

Then follow up by asking the participants: Have you pre-identified locations for incident facilities?

Note that participants might not know, but that they should ask their supervisors/leadership.

Visual 3.29

Incident Facilities: Summary

- A single Incident Command Post should be established on all incidents—even small ones!
- Incidents may require additional facilities (e.g., a call center).
- Areas may be predesignated incident facilities for the surrounding community (e.g., shelters, staging areas, helibases, medical centers).

FEMA

Visual 3.29
ICS Features and Principles

Instructor Notes: Present the following key points

A single Incident Command Post should be established on all incidents, even on a small incident.

Incidents may require additional facilities beyond those that are standard ICS facilities.

Areas may be predesignated incident facilities for the surrounding community (e.g., shelters, Staging Areas, Helibases, medical centers).

Visual 3.30

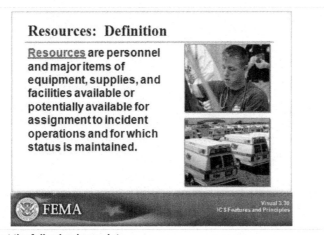

Instructor Notes: Present the following key points

In ICS, resources include personnel and major items of equipment, supplies, and facilities available or potentially available for assignment to incident operations and for which status is maintained.

Visual 3.31

Instructor Notes: Present the following key points

As mentioned in the previous unit, resources at an incident must be managed effectively. Maintaining an accurate and up-to-date picture of resource utilization is a critical component of incident management. Resource management includes processes for

- Categorizing, credentialing, and identifying resources in advance.
- Ordering resources.
- Dispatching resources.
- Tracking resources.
- Recovering resources.

Resource management also includes processes for reimbursement for resources, as appropriate.

Visual 3.32

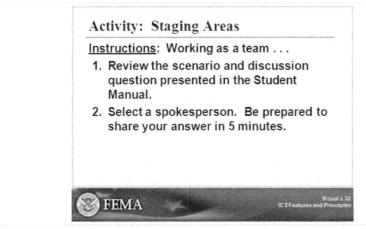

Instructor Notes: Present the following key points

Activity Purpose: To reinforce participants' understanding of Staging Areas and resource management.

Instructions: Working as a team:

1. Review the scenario and discussion question presented in the Student Manual.
2. Select a spokesperson. Be prepared to share your answer in 5 minutes.

Time: 10 minutes

Debrief Instructions:

1. Monitor the time. Notify the participants when 2 minutes remain.
2. Have each spokesperson present their team's answers.

Scenario: A bomb threat has been made at a local business.

Ask the participants: Where would you establish a Staging Area?

Acknowledge the participants' responses. There is no single correct response. If not mentioned by the participants, note that the location of the Staging Area should take into consideration factors such as access, site security, and communications.

Communications and Information Management

Visual 3.33

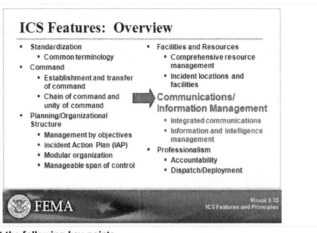

Instructor Notes: Present the following key points

The next part of this unit covers communications and information management, including:

- Integrated communications.
- Information and intelligence management.

Visual 3.34

Instructor Notes: Present the following key points

Incident communications are facilitated through:

- The development and use of a common communications plan.
- The interoperability of communication equipment, procedures, and systems.

A common communications plan is essential for ensuring that responders can communicate with one another during an incident. Before an incident, it is critical to develop an integrated voice and data communications system (equipment, systems, and protocols).

Visual 3.35

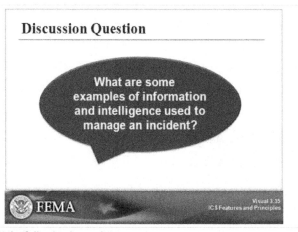

Instructor Notes: Present the following key points

The analysis and sharing of information and intelligence is an important component of ICS. Incident management must establish a process for gathering, sharing, and managing incident-related information and intelligence.

Ask the participants: What are some examples of information and intelligence used to manage an incident?

If not mentioned by the participants, add the following items:

Intelligence includes other operational information that may come from a variety of different sources, such as:

- Weather forecasts.
- Planned events.
- Structural plans and vulnerabilities.
- Jurisdiction's hazard/risk/vulnerability assessments.
- Threats, including potential violence.
- Surveillance of disease outbreak.

Visual 3.36

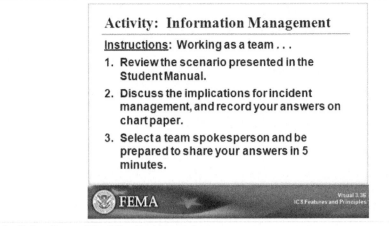

Instructor Notes: Present the following key points

Activity Purpose: To reinforce participants' understanding of managing incident information and intelligence.

Instructions: Working as a team:

1. Review the scenario presented in the Student Manual.
2. Discuss the implications for incident management, and record your answers on chart paper.
3. Select a team spokesperson and be prepared to share your answers in 5 minutes.

Time: 10 minutes

Debrief Instructions:

1. Monitor the time. Notify the participants when 2 minutes remain.
2. Have each spokesperson present their team's answers.

Scenario: Continuing severe weather is causing widespread damage. 9-1-1 operators are receiving conflicting reports about life-safety needs, including a possible structural collapse of an assisted living facility.

Ask the participants: What lessons learned could be applied to managing incident information and intelligence?

If not mentioned by the group, explain that, without accurate information and intelligence, responders may find it difficult to:

- Take measures to ensure the safety of responders.
- Prioritize needs.
- Determine incident objectives.
- Identify the resources needed.

Professionalism

Visual 3.37

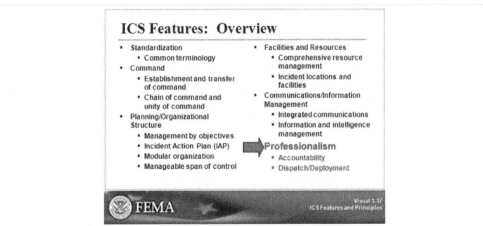

Instructor Notes: Present the following key points

The last part of this unit covers professionalism, including:

- Accountability.
- Dispatch/deployment.

Visual 3.38

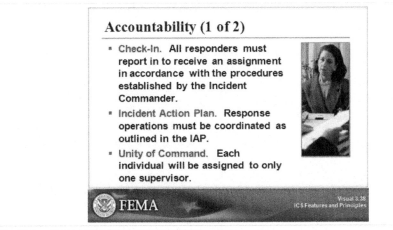

Instructor Notes: Present the following key points

Effective accountability during incident operations is essential. Individuals must abide by their institutional policies and guidelines and any applicable local, State, or Federal rules and regulations.

The following principles must be adhered to:

- Check-In. All responders must report in to receive an assignment in accordance with the procedures established by the Incident Commander.
- Incident Action Plan. Response operations must be coordinated as outlined in the IAP.
- Unity of Command. Each individual will be assigned to only one supervisor.

The next visual includes additional principles that must be adhered to.

Visual 3.39

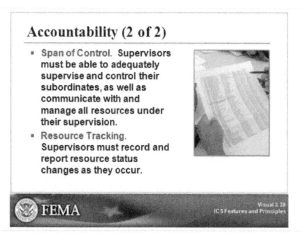

Instructor Notes: Present the following key points

- Span of Control. Supervisors must be able to adequately supervise and control their subordinates, as well as communicate with and manage all resources under their supervision.
- Resource Tracking. Supervisors must record and report resource status changes as they occur.

Visual 3.40

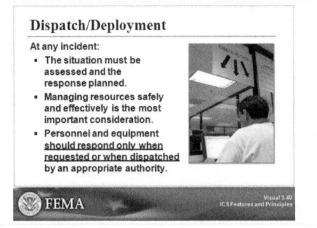

Instructor Notes: Present the following key points

Another key feature of ICS is the importance of managing resources to adjust to changing conditions.

When an incident occurs, you must be dispatched or deployed to become part of the incident response. In other words, until you are deployed to the incident organization, you remain in your everyday role.

After being deployed, your first task is to check in and receive an assignment.

After check-in, you will locate your incident supervisor and obtain your initial briefing. The briefings you receive and give should include:

- Current assessment of the situation.
- Identification of your specific job responsibilities.
- Identification of coworkers.
- Location of work area.
- Identification of break areas, as appropriate.
- Procedural instructions for obtaining needed resources.
- Operational periods/work shifts.
- Required safety procedures and personal protective equipment (PPE), as appropriate.

Visual 3.41

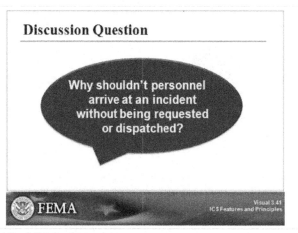

Instructor Notes: Present the following key points

Ask the participants: Why shouldn't personnel arrive at an incident without being requested or dispatched?

Acknowledge the participants' responses. If not mentioned by the participants, add the following points:

- Uncontrolled and uncoordinated arrival of resources at emergencies causes significant accountability issues.
- Self-dispatched or freelancing resources cause safety risks to responders, civilians, and others who are operating within the parameters of the Incident Action Plan.
- Chaos at the scene occurs, creating additional risks.
- Emergency access routes can be blocked, preventing trained responders from gaining access to the site or not allowing critically injured personnel to be transported from the scene.

In the World Trade Center 9/11 response, many volunteers self-dispatched, undermining command and control at the scene and clogging the streets so that other responders assigned to the WTC had difficulty getting through.

The bottom line is that when resources show up that have not been requested, the incident management system may fail.

Visual 3.42

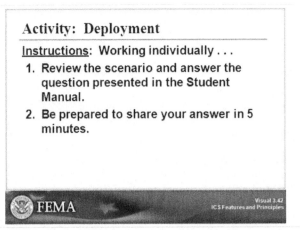

Instructor Notes: Present the following key points

Activity Purpose: To reinforce the participants' understanding of the importance of dispatch and deployment.

Instructions: Working individually:

- Review the scenario and discussion question presented in the Student Manual.
- Be prepared to share your answer in 5 minutes.

Time: 10 minutes

Debrief Instructions:

1. Monitor the time. Notify the participants when 2 minutes remain.
2. Ask for volunteers to present their answers.

Scenario: Rosa is an off-duty certified Emergency Medical Technician who lives near the scene of a major structural collapse that has occurred in a busy shopping center. The media are reporting that there are injured people wandering around the parking area who need immediate medical attention.

Ask the participants: What should Rosa do?

Acknowledge the participants' responses. If not mentioned by the participants, mention that:

- Rosa should report her whereabouts to dispatch and wait for deployment to the scene.
- Rosa should not immediately rush to the scene.

Unit Summary

Visual 3.43

Summary (1 of 2)

ICS:

- Utilizes management features including the use of common terminology and a modular organizational structure.
- Emphasizes effective planning through the use of management by objectives and Incident Action Plans.
- Supports responders by providing data they need through effective information and intelligence management.

FEMA

Visual 3.43
ICS Features and Principles

Instructor Notes: Present the following key points

ICS:

- Utilizes management features including the use of common terminology and a modular organizational structure.
- Emphasizes effective planning through the use of management by objectives and Incident Action Plans.
- Supports responders by providing data they need through effective information and intelligence management.

Visual 3.44

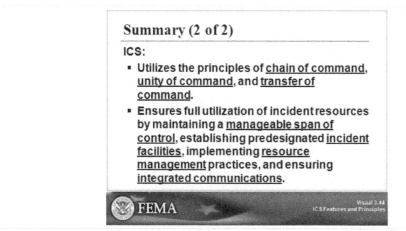

Instructor Notes: Present the following key points

ICS:

- Utilizes the principles of chain of command, unity of command, and transfer of command.
- Ensures full utilization of incident resources by maintaining a manageable span of control, establishing predesignated incident facilities, implementing resource management practices, and ensuring integrated communications.

Ask if anyone has any questions about content covered in this unit.

The next unit will cover the Incident Commander and Command Staff functions.

UNIT 4: INCIDENT COMMANDER AND COMMAND STAFF FUNCTIONS

This page intentionally left blank

Unit Objectives

At the end of this unit, the participants should be able to:

- Identify the five major ICS management functions.
- Identify the position titles associated with the Command Staff.
- Describe the role and function of the Incident Commander.
- Describe the role and function of the Command Staff.

Scope

- Unit Introduction
- Incident Commander
- Command Staff
- Unit Summary

Methodology

The instructors will outline the objectives for this unit. The instructors will overview the management functions that are part of every incident, and will then overview the role of the Incident Commander. Next, the instructors will summarize the Incident Commander's responsibilities. The participants will then answer a question about the responsibilities at an incident scene. The instructors will introduce the role of the Deputy Incident Commander.

Next, the instructors will transition to the Command Staff. The presentation outlines the responsibilities of the Public Information Officer, Safety Officer, and Liaison Officer. The participants will watch a video that will provide an overview of the Command Staff Officers. The instructors will then lead an activity in which the participants apply the roles of the Command Staff to a scenario. To summarize the unit, the instructors will review the unit objectives and then transition to Unit 5.

Materials

- PowerPoint visuals 4.1 – 4.18
- Instructor Guide
- PowerPoint slides and a computer display system
- Student Manual

Time Plan

A suggested time plan for this unit is shown below. More or less time may be required, based on the experience level of the group.

Topic	Time
Unit Introduction	5 minutes
Incident Commander	15 minutes
Command Staff	15 minutes
Activity: Command Staff Roles	15 minutes
Unit Summary	5 minutes
Total Time	55 minutes

Unit Introduction

Visual 4.1

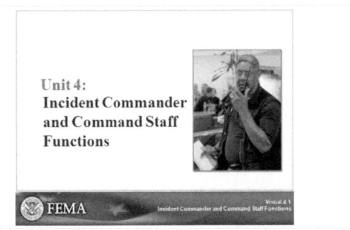

Instructor Notes: Present the following key points

This unit will provide an overview of the role of the Incident Commander and Command Staff, including these topics:

- Five major management functions
- Incident Commander roles and responsibilities
- Command Staff roles and responsibilities

Visual 4.2

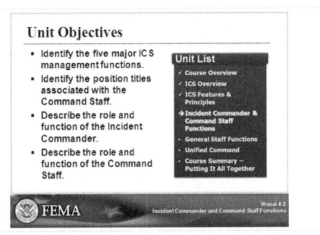

Instructor Notes: Present the following key points

By the end of this unit you should be able to:

- Identify the five major ICS management functions.
- Identify the position titles associated with the Command Staff.
- Describe the role and function of the Incident Commander.
- Describe the role and function of the Command Staff.

Visual 4.3

Management Function Descriptions

Function	Description
Incident Command	• Establishes incident objectives, strategies, and priorities. • Assume overall responsibility for the incident.
Operations	• Determines tactics and resources for achieving objectives. • Directs the tactical response.
Planning	• Collects and analyzes information. • Tracks resources. • Maintains documentation.
Logistics	• Provides resources and needed services.
Finance/Administration	• Accounts for expenditures, claims, and compensation. • Procures needed resources.

FEMA

Visual 4.3
Incident Commander and Command Staff Functions

Instructor Notes: Present the following key points

Every incident requires that certain management functions be performed. The problem must be identified and assessed, a plan to deal with it developed and implemented, and the necessary resources procured and paid for. Regardless of the size of the incident, these management functions still will apply.

There are five major management functions that are the foundation upon which the ICS organization develops. These functions are:

Incident Command	Sets the incident objectives, strategies, and priorities and has overall responsibility for the incident.
Operations	Conducts operations to reach the incident objectives. Establishes the tactics and directs all operational resources.
Planning	Supports the incident action planning process by tracking resources, collecting/analyzing information, and maintaining documentation.
Logistics	Provides resources and needed services to support the achievement of the incident objectives.
Finance & Administration	Monitors costs related to the incident. Provides accounting, procurement, time recording, and cost analyses.

Incident Commander

Visual 4.4

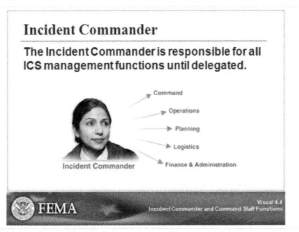

Instructor Notes: Present the following key points

The Incident Commander has overall responsibility for managing the incident by establishing objectives, planning strategies, and implementing tactics.

The Incident Commander is the only position that is always staffed in ICS applications. On small incidents and events, one person, the Incident Commander, may accomplish all management functions.

The Incident Commander is responsible for all ICS management functions until he or she delegates those functions.

Visual 4.5

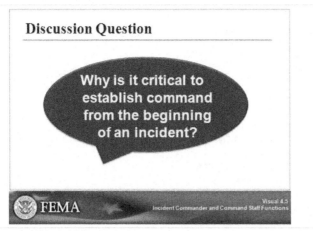

Instructor Notes: Present the following key points

Ask the participants: Why is it critical to establish command from the beginning of an incident?

If not mentioned by the participants, add the following key points:

- Lack of command becomes a safety hazard for responders and others.
- Size-up and decision-making are impossible without a command structure.
- It is difficult to expand a disorganized organization if the incident escalates.

Emphasize that all incident responses begin by establishing command.

Visual 4.6

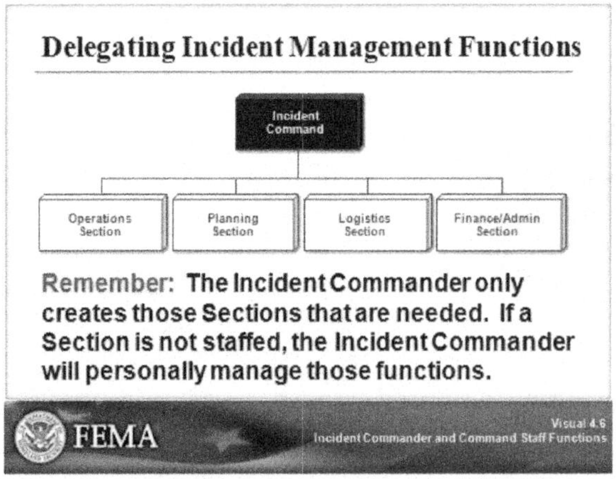

Delegating Incident Management Functions

Incident Command

| Operations Section | Planning Section | Logistics Section | Finance/Admin Section |

Remember: The Incident Commander only creates those Sections that are needed. If a Section is not staffed, the Incident Commander will personally manage those functions.

FEMA

Visual 4.6
Incident Commander and Command Staff Functions

Instructor Notes: Present the following key points

The ICS organization is modular and has the capability to expand or contract to meet the needs of the incident. On a larger incident, the Incident Commander may create Sections and delegate the Operations, Planning, Logistics, and Finance/Administration functions.

Visual 4.7

Incident Commander Responsibilities

The Incident Commander is responsible for:

- Ensuring incident safety.
- Providing information to internal and external stakeholders.
- Establishing and maintaining liaison with other agencies participating in the incident.

FEMA

Visual 4.7
Incident Commander and Command Staff Functions

Instructor Notes: Present the following key points

The Incident Commander is specifically responsible for:

- Ensuring incident safety.
- Providing information to internal and external stakeholders.
- Establishing and maintaining liaison with other agencies participating in the incident.

These are critical functions and, until delegated, are the responsibility of the Incident Commander.

The Incident Commander may appoint one or more Deputies. Deputy Incident Commanders must be as qualified as the Incident Commander.

Visual 4.8

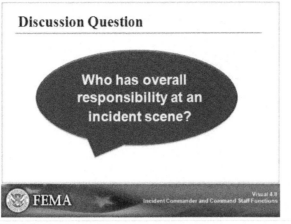

Instructor Notes: Present the following key points

Ask the participants: Who has overall responsibility at an incident scene?

Acknowledge the participants' answers. If not mentioned by the participants, explain that the correct answer is that the Incident Commander has overall responsibility at an incident scene.

Then follow up by asking the participants: What is the role of agency executives?

Acknowledge the participants' responses. If not mentioned, explain that agency executives provide the following to the Incident Commander:

- Policy
- Mission
- Direction
- Authority

Visual 4.9

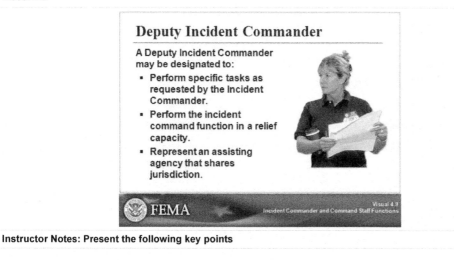

Instructor Notes: Present the following key points

A Deputy Incident Commander may be designated to:

- Perform specific tasks as requested by the Incident Commander.
- Perform the incident command function in a relief capacity.
- Represent an assisting agency that shares jurisdiction.

If a Deputy is assigned, he or she must be fully qualified to assume the Incident Commander's position.

Visual 4.10

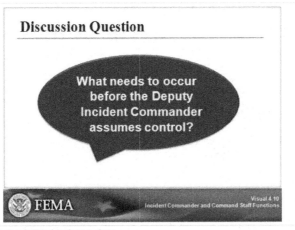

Instructor Notes: Present the following key points

Ask the participants: What needs to occur before the Deputy Commander can assume control for the next operational period?

Acknowledge the participants' responses. If not mentioned, tell the participants that the correct answer is that before the Deputy Incident Commander can assume control for the next operational period, there must be a transfer of command briefing and notification to all personnel that a change in command is taking place.

Command Staff

Visual 4.11

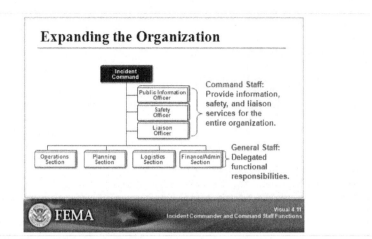

Instructor Notes: Present the following key points

As incidents grow, the Incident Commander may delegate authority for performance of certain activities to the Command Staff and the General Staff.

The Incident Commander should add positions only as needed.

Visual 4.12

Instructor Notes: Present the following key points

The following video will provide an overview of the Command Staff Officers.

Video Transcript:

You've now learned that the Incident Commander has overall authority and responsibility for conducting incident operations. An Incident Commander may assign staff to assist with managing the incident.

The Command Staff consists of the Public Information Officer, Safety Officer, and Liaison Officer, who all report directly to the Incident Commander.

Let's look at the roles of each member of the Command Staff. The Public Information Officer serves as the conduit for information to internal and external stakeholders, including the media and the public.

Accurate information is essential. The Public Information Officer serves as the primary contact for anyone who wants information about the incident and the response to it.

Another member of the Command Staff is the Safety Officer, who monitors conditions and develops measures for assuring the safety of all personnel.

The Safety Officer is responsible for advising the Incident Commander on issues regarding incident safety, conducting risk analyses, and implementing safety measures.

The final member of the Command Staff is the Liaison Officer, who serves as the primary contact for supporting agencies assisting at an incident.

Additionally, the Liaison Officer responds to requests from incident personnel for contacts among the assisting and cooperating agencies, and monitors incident operations in order to identify any current or potential problems between response agencies.

A Command Staff may not be necessary at every incident, but every incident requires that certain management functions be performed. An effective Command Staff frees the Incident Commander to assume a leadership role.

Visual 4.13

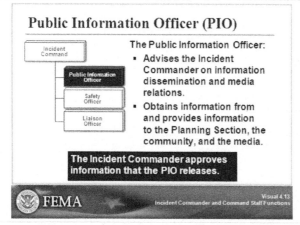

Instructor Notes: Present the following key points

The Public Information Officer (PIO):

- Advises the Incident Commander on information dissemination and media relations. Note that the Incident Commander approves information that the PIO releases.
- Obtains information from and provides information to the Planning Section.
- Obtains information from and provides information to the community and media.

Visual 4.14

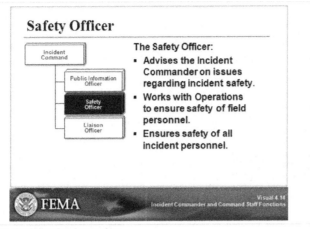

Instructor Notes: Present the following key points

The Safety Officer:

- Advises the Incident Commander on issues regarding incident safety.
- Works with the Operations Section to ensure safety of field personnel.
- Ensures the safety of all incident personnel.

Visual 4.15

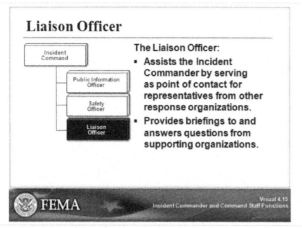

Instructor Notes: Present the following key points

The Liaison Officer:

- Assists the Incident Commander by serving as a point of contact for representatives from other response organizations.
- Provides briefings to and answer questions from supporting organizations.

Visual 4.16

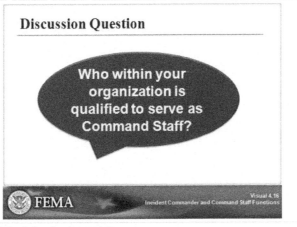

Instructor Notes: Present the following key points

Ask the participants: Who within your organization is qualified to serve as Command Staff?

Acknowledge the participants' responses. If necessary, remind the participants that the following personnel comprise the Command Staff:

- Public Information Officer, who serves as the conduit for information to internal and external stakeholders, including the media or parents.
- Safety Officer, who monitors safety conditions and develops measures for assuring the safety of all response personnel.
- Liaison Officer, who serves as the primary contact for supporting agencies assisting at an incident.

Visual 4.17

Activity: Command Staff Roles

Instructions: Working as a team . . .

1. Review the case study presented in your Student Manual.
2. Identify which Command Staff positions would be assigned.
3. Next, determine what specific activities the Incident Commander would delegate to each Command Staff member.
4. Select a spokesperson. Be prepared to present in 10 minutes.

FEMA

Visual 4.17
Incident Commander and Command Staff Functions

Instructor Notes: Present the following key points

Activity Purpose: To illustrate how ICS can be used to address incident management issues.

Instructions: Working as a team:

1. Review the scenario presented on the next page of your Student Manual.
2. Identify which Command Staff positions would be assigned.
3. Next, if you were the Incident Commander, what specific activities would you delegate to each Command Staff member?
4. Select a spokesperson. Be prepared to present in 10 minutes.

Time: 15 minutes

Instructor Debrief Instructions:

1. Monitor the time. Notify the participants when 5 minutes remain.
2. When 10 minutes have passed, ask the spokesperson from each group to present their Command Staff positions assigned and the activities that were delegated.

Scenario:

An unexpected flash flood has struck a small community. As a result:

- Homes, schools, the business district, and the community college are being evacuated.
- Damage to critical infrastructure includes contamination of the water supply, downed power lines, and damaged roads.
- Perimeter control and security in the business district are needed.
- Mutual aid is arriving from several surrounding communities.
- Media representatives are arriving at the scene.

Questions:

1. Which Command Staff positions would be assigned?
2. If you were the Incident Commander, what specific activities would you delegate to each Command Staff member?

Acknowledge the groups' responses. If not mentioned by the group, add the following potential activities:

- Public Information Officer: Work with the media to ensure that evacuation orders are communicated to affected neighbors. Prepare releases with information about the status of the business district prior to the next morning. Arrange a press briefing in advance of the next news cycle.
- Liaison Officer: Coordinate with communities that are providing mutual aid and with private-sector utilities that are supporting the response. Work with the business community to identify response needs.
- Safety Officer: Ensure the safety of incident personnel from contaminated waste water, electrical hazards, and fatigue.

Unit Summary

Visual 4.18

Summary

Are you now able to:

- Identify the five major ICS management functions?
- Identify the position titles associated with the Command Staff?
- Describe the role and function of the Incident Commander?
- Describe the role and function of the Command Staff?

FEMA

Visual 4.18
Incident Commander and Command Staff Functions

Instructor Notes: Present the following key points

Are you now able to:

- Identify the five major ICS management functions?
- Identify the position titles associated with the Command Staff?
- Describe the role and function of the Incident Commander?
- Describe the role and function of the Command Staff?

Answer any questions the participants might have about this unit.

The next unit will discuss the roles and responsibilities of the General Staff.

UNIT 5: GENERAL STAFF FUNCTIONS

This page intentionally left blank

Unit Objectives

At the end of this unit, the participants should be able to describe the roles and functions of the General Staff, including the:

- Operations Section.
- Planning Section.
- Logistics Section.
- Finance/Administration Section.

Scope

- Unit Introduction
- General Staff
- Operations Section
- Planning Section
- Logistics Section
- Finance and Administration Section
- Unit Summary

Methodology

The instructors will outline this unit's objective. They will then explain that as incidents expand, there may be need to add supervisory layers to the organization structure. This unit will describe these layers in depth and, specifically, will explain the role of the General Staff in the ICS structure.

The instructors will then explain the importance of using specific ICS position titles. They will identify the titles for all ICS supervisory levels.

The instructors will start with the Operations Section. The participants will then watch a video describing the responsibilities of each Section Chief. The instructors will further explain the Operations Section. The instructors will further explain the role of Task Forces, Strike Teams, and Single Resources. The participants will complete an activity applying how the Operation Section can be organized into teams.

The instructors will then overview the key Planning Section tasks, and discuss the roles of the four Planning Section Units. They will also explain the use of Technical Specialists. The participants will complete a Knowledge Review matching particular Planning Section Units to specific functions.

The instructors will then identify the tasks of the Logistics Section. The instructors will describe the Service Branch and the Support Branch and their corresponding Units.

The instructors will then outline the major tasks of the Finance/Administration Section. The instructors will describe each of the four Finance/Administration Section Units.

The participants will then complete an activity that allows them to apply the information they have learned about Section Chief roles and responsibilities.

To summarize the unit, the instructors will present a scenario-based activity in which the participants must answer questions that assess their understanding of the role of the General Staff. After discussing the questions based on the scenario, the instructors will ask the participants if they have met the learning objective for this unit.

Materials

- PowerPoint visuals 5.1 – 5.30
- Instructor Guide
- PowerPoint slides and a computer display system
- Student Manual

Time Plan

A suggested time plan for this unit is shown below. More or less time may be required, based on the experience level of the group.

Topic	Time
Unit Introduction	5 minutes
General Staff	10 minutes
Operations Section	15 minutes
Activity: Operations Section	20 minutes
Activity: Organizing the Ops Section	10 minutes
Planning Section	10 minutes
Activity: Planning Section Units	10 minutes
Logistics Section	10 minutes
Finance and Administration Section	10 minutes
Activity: Section Chiefs	10 minutes
Activity: General Staff Functions	20 minutes
Unit Summary	5 minutes

Topic	Time
Total Time	2 hours, 5 minutes

Unit Introduction

Visual 5.1

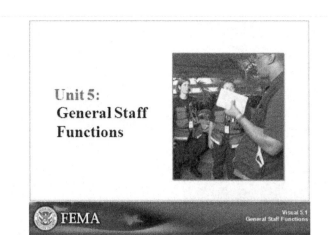

Instructor Notes: Present the following key points

This unit will provide an overview of ICS General Staff functions, including the following topics:

- Operations Section
- Planning Section
- Logistics Section
- Finance/Administration Section

The unit concludes with an activity in which you will apply what you have learned about the General Staff.

Visual 5.2

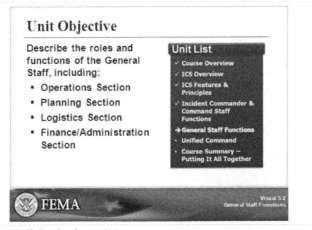

Instructor Notes: Present the following key points

By the end of this unit, you should be able to describe the roles and functions of the General Staff, including the:

- Operations Section
- Planning Section
- Logistics Section
- Finance/Administration Section

Most incidents usually are small, managed in a short period of time, and require few outside response resources. However, an institution may become involved in a larger incident affecting the whole community and may be isolated. In such cases, a larger ICS organization may be required to manage the incident.

General Staff

Visual 5.3

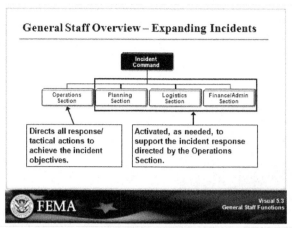

Instructor Notes: Present the following key points

The General Staff overall responsibilities are summarized in the graphic. In an expanding incident, the Incident Command first establishes the Operations Section. The remaining Sections are established as needed to support the operation.

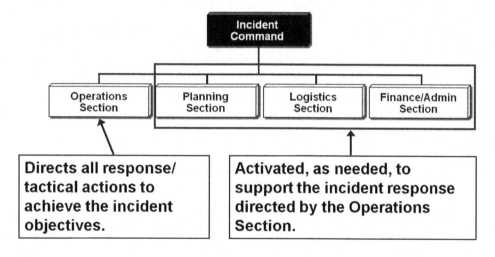

Visual 5.4

Instructor Notes: Present the following key points

The definitions of ICS organizational components are shown in the Student Manual. Later, you will learn more about the different organizational elements.

- Sections: The organizational levels with responsibility for a major functional area of the incident (e.g., Operations, Planning, Logistics, Finance/Administration). The person in charge of each Section is designated as a Chief.
- Divisions: Used to divide an incident geographically. The person in charge of each Division is designated as a Supervisor.
- Groups: Used to describe functional areas of operation. The person in charge of each Group is designated as a Supervisor.
- Branches: Used when the number of Divisions or Groups exceeds the span of control. Can be either geographical or functional. The person in charge of each Branch is designated as a Director.
- Task Forces: A combination of mixed resources with common communications operating under the direct supervision of a Task Force Leader.
- Strike Teams: A set number of resources of the same kind and type with common communications operating under the direct supervision of a Strike Team Leader.
- Single Resources: May be individuals, a piece of equipment and its personnel complement, or a crew or team of individuals with an identified supervisor that can be used at an incident.

Visual 5.5

ICS Supervisory Position Titles

Organizational Level	Supervisor Title	Support Position Title
Incident Command	Incident Commander	Deputy
Command Staff	Officer	Assistant
General Staff (Section)	Chief	Deputy
Branch	Director	Deputy
Division/Group	Supervisor	N/A
Unit	Leader	Manager
Strike Team/Task Force	Leader	Single Resource Boss

FEMA

Visual 5.5
General Staff Functions

Instructor Notes: Present the following key points

Additional levels of supervision are added as the ICS organization expands. The ICS supervisory titles are shown in the graphic.

Organizational Level	Supervisor Title	Support Position Title
Incident Command	Incident Commander	Deputy
Command Staff	Officer	Assistant
General Staff (Section)	Chief	Deputy
Branch	Director	Deputy
Division/Group	Supervisor	N/A
Unit	Leader	Manager
Strike Team/Task Force	Leader	Single Resource Boss

Visual 5.6

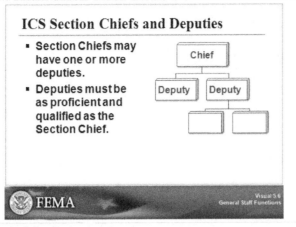

Instructor Notes: Present the following key points

As mentioned previously, the person in charge of each Section is designated as a Chief. Section Chiefs have the ability to expand their Sections to meet the needs of the situation.

Each of the Section Chiefs may have a Deputy, or more than one, if necessary. The Deputy:

- May assume responsibility for a specific portion of the primary position, work as relief, or be assigned other tasks.
- Must be as proficient as the person for whom he or she works.

Visual 5.7

Click on the image to start the video.

Instructor Notes: Present the following key points

The following video will provide an overview of the General Staff Sections.

Video Transcript:

As you previously learned, an Incident Commander is responsible for all incident management functions including: operations, planning, logistics, and finance and administration.

Depending on the incident needs, the Incident Commander may delegate some or all of these functions by establishing Sections. If a Section Chief is assigned to an incident, he or she will report directly to the Incident Commander.

Together, these Section Chiefs are referred to as the General Staff. Let's take a look at the responsibilities of each Section Chief.

The Operations Section Chief is responsible for developing and implementing strategy and tactics to accomplish the incident objectives. This means that the Operations Section Chief organizes, assigns, and supervises all the tactical or response resources assigned to the incident. Additionally, if a Staging Area is established, the Operations Section Chief would manage it.

The Planning Section Chief oversees the collection, evaluation, and dissemination of operational information related to the incident. It is the Planning Section's responsibility to prepare and disseminate the Incident Action Plan, as well as track the status of all incident resources.

The Planning Section helps ensure responders have accurate information and provides resources such as maps and floor plans.

The Logistics Section is responsible for providing facilities, services, and material support for the incident.

Logistics is critical on more complex incidents. The Logistics Section Chief assists the Incident Commander and Operations Section Chief by providing the resources and services required to support incident activities. During an incident, Logistics is responsible for ensuring the well- being of responders by providing sufficient food, water, and medical services. Logistics is also responsible for arranging communication equipment, computers, transportation, and anything else needed to support the incident.

Another critical function during complex incidents is Finance and Administration.

The Finance and Administration Section Chief is responsible for all of the financial and cost analysis aspects of an incident. These include contract negotiation, recording personnel and equipment time, documenting and processing claims for accidents and injuries occurring at the incident, and keeping a running tally of the costs associated with the incident.

We've now introduced you to the four ICS Sections.

It is important to remember that the ICS organizational structure is determined based on the incident objectives and resource requirements. It expands and contracts in a flexible manner. And, only those functions, positions, or Sections necessary for a particular incident are filled.

Visual 5.8

Increasing Interagency Coordination

When an incident involves multiple organizations, assigning Deputies from other organizations can increase interagency coordination.

Incident Commander

Operations Section Chief

Deputy Operations Section Chief

FEMA

Visual 5.8
General Staff Functions

Instructor Notes: Present the following key points

When an incident involves multiple organizations, assigning Deputies from other organizations can increase interagency coordination.

For example, for the response to a hazardous materials incident, public works, law enforcement, and hazmat responders might work together, with one agency taking the lead and representatives from the other organizations serving as deputies.

Operations Section

Visual 5.9

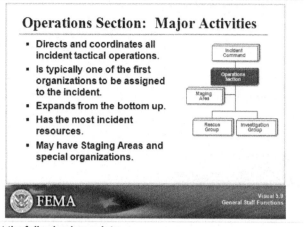

Instructor Notes: Present the following key points

The Operations Section is responsible for directing and coordinating all incident tactical operations.

The Operations Section:

- Is typically one of the first organizations to be assigned to the incident.
- Develops from the bottom up.
- Has the most incident resources.
- May have Staging Areas and special organizations.

Visual 5.10

Operations: Single Resources

On a smaller incident, the Operations Section may be comprised of an Operations Section Chief and single resources.

Operations Section Chief — Industrial Hygienist — Facility Engineer — IT Specialist

FEMA

Visual 5.10
General Staff Functions

Instructor Notes: Present the following key points

Single resources are individuals, a piece of equipment and its personnel complement, or a crew or team of individuals with an identified supervisor. On a smaller incident, the Operations Section may be comprised of an Operations Section Chief and single resources.

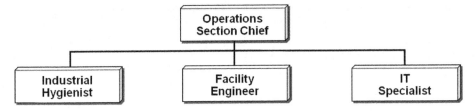

Visual 5.11

Operations: Teams

Single resources may be organized into teams. Using standard ICS terminology, the two types of team configurations are:

- Task Forces, which are a <u>combination of mixed resources</u> with common communications supervised by a Leader.
- Strike Teams, which include all <u>similar resources</u> with common communications supervised by a Leader.

FEMA

Visual 5.11
General Staff Functions

Instructor Notes: Present the following key points

Single resources may be organized into teams. Using standard ICS terminology, the two types of team configurations are:

- Task Forces, which are a combination of mixed resources with common communications operating under the direct supervision of a Leader.
- Strike Teams, which include all similar resources with common communications operating under the direct supervision of a Leader.

Visual 5.12

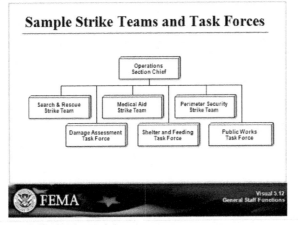

Instructor Notes: Present the following key points

The Operations Section organization chart shows possible team assignments during an incident. Each team would have a Team Leader reporting to the Operations Section Chief.

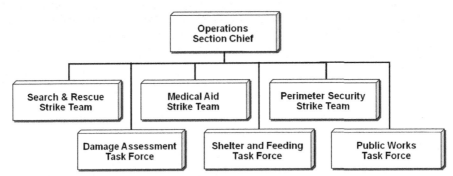

These are examples of possible strike teams and task forces. Strike teams and task forces should be established based on the type of incident and unique requirements of the area.

Ask the participants: What other strike teams and task forces might you use during a response?

Visual 5.13

Activity: Operations Section

<u>Instructions:</u> Working as a team . . .

1. Review the scenario presented in the Student Manual.
2. Develop an organization chart depicting how the <u>Operations Section</u> could be organized into teams.
3. List the responsibilities of each team.
4. Be prepared to present in 15 minutes.

FEMA

Visual 5.13
General Staff Functions

Instructor Notes: Present the following key points

Activity Purpose: To reinforce participants' understanding of how Operations Sections are organized.

Instructions: Working as a team:

1. Review the scenario presented in the Student Manual.
2. Develop an organization chart depicting how the Operations Section could be organized into teams. Draw the team structure on chart paper as large as possible.
3. List the responsibilities of each team.
4. Be prepared to present in 15 minutes.

Time: 20 minutes

Instructor Debrief Instructions:

1. Monitor the time. Notify the participants when 5 minutes remain.
2. Ask for volunteers to present their group's answers.

Scenario: Heavy rains have caused flash flooding. Your jurisdiction is effectively isolated by the flood waters and damage. It may be several hours before mutual aid resources arrive.

Instructor Note: There is no single correct answer. Have the teams hang up their charts on one wall. Compare the similarities and differences among the team structures

Visual 5.14

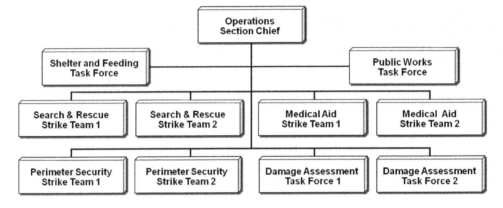

Instructor Notes: Present the following key points

To maintain span of control, each team should be comprised of a Team Leader and no more than 5 to 7 team members.

Ask the participants: As teams are added, what happens to the Operations Section Chief's span of control?

Visual 5.15

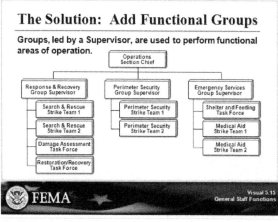

Instructor Notes: Present the following key points

On a large, complex incident the Operations Section may become very large. Using the ICS principle of modular organization, the Operations Section may add elements to manage span of control. Groups are used to perform functional areas of operation. The organization chart below illustrates how Groups can be used to maintain span of control within the Operations Section.

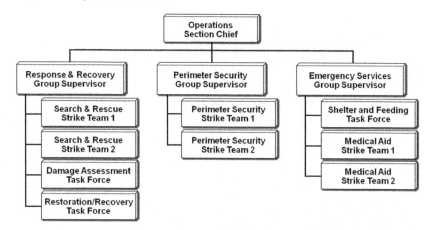

Visual 5.16

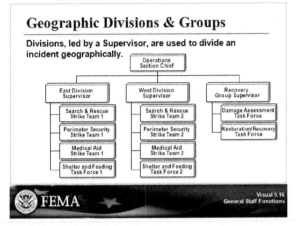

Instructor Notes: Present the following key points

Divisions can be used to add a level of supervision. Divisions are used to divide an incident geographically. The organization chart below illustrates how Groups and Divisions can be used together to maintain span of control within the Operations Section. The use of Divisions would be effective if the incident covered a large or isolated area.

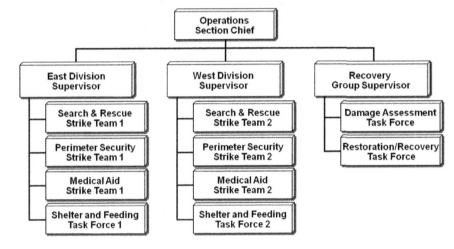

Visual 5.17

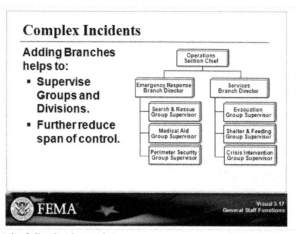

Instructor Notes: Present the following key points

The Operations Section Chief may add Branches to supervise Groups and Divisions and further reduce his or her span of control. The person in charge of each Branch is designated as a Director.

Review the chart. Ask the participants: What are the advantages of reducing the Operations Section Chief's span of control?

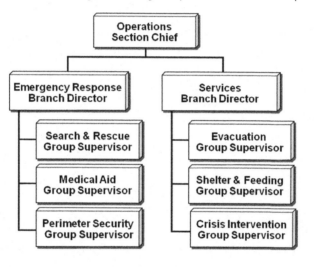

Visual 5.18

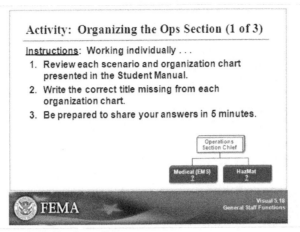

Instructor Notes: Present the following key points

Activity Purpose: To reinforce the participants' understanding of Groups and Divisions in the Operations Section.

Instructions: Working individually:

1. Review each scenario and organization chart presented in the Student Manual.
2. Write the correct title missing from each organization chart.
3. Be prepared to share your answers in 5 minutes.

Time: 10 minutes

Debrief Instructions:

1. Monitor the time. Notify the participants when 2 minutes remain.
2. Ask for volunteers to present their group's answers.

Scenario 1: As incident objectives and resources expand, the Operations Section Chief begins organizing resources into functional areas. What title is the correct addition to the organization chart?

- Unit Supervisor
- Team Supervisor
- Group Supervisor

The correct addition to the organization chart is: Group Supervisor.

Groups are used to describe functional areas of operations. The person in charge of each Group is designated as a Supervisor.

Visual 5.19

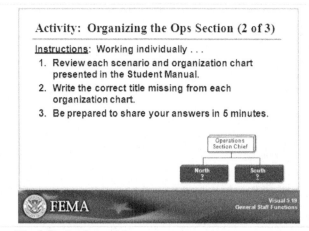

Instructor Notes: Present the following key points

Scenario 2: The incident has isolated one part of the area. Given this isolation, the Operations Section Chief has decided to organize resources by geographical areas. What title is the correct addition to the organization chart?

- Task Force Supervisor
- Division Supervisor
- Sector Supervisor

Provide feedback on the question:

The correct addition to the organization chart is: Division Supervisor.

Divisions are used to divide an incident geographically. The person in charge of each Division is designated as a Supervisor.

Visual 5.20

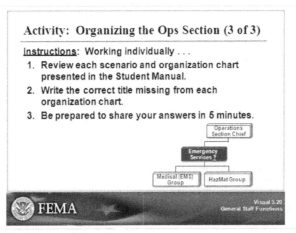

Instructor Notes: Present the following key points

Scenario 3: As the incident expands even further, the Operations Section Chief determines that there is a need to add another level of supervision to manage the Groups. What title is the correct addition to the organization chart?

- Branch Director
- Department Director
- Field Director

Provide feedback on the question:

The correct addition to the organization chart is: Branch Director.

Branches may be added when the number of Divisions or Groups exceeds the span of control, and can be either geographical or functional. The person in charge of each Branch is designated as a Director.

The next section of this unit covers the Planning Section.

Planning Section

Visual 5.21

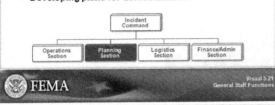

Instructor Notes: Present the following key points

The major activities of the Planning Section may include:

- Collecting, evaluating, and displaying incident intelligence and information.
- Preparing and documenting Incident Action Plans.
- Tracking resources assigned to the incident.
- Maintaining incident documentation.
- Developing plans for demobilization.

Visual 5.22

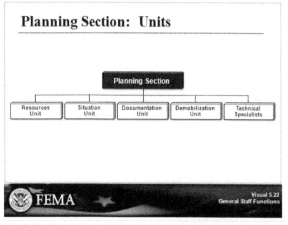

Instructor Notes: Present the following key points

The Planning Section can be further staffed with four Units. In addition, Technical Specialists who provide special expertise useful in incident management and response may also be assigned to work in the Planning Section. Depending on the needs, Technical Specialists may also be assigned to other Sections in the organization.

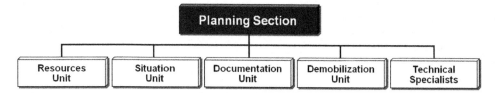

- Resources Unit: Conducts all check-in activities and maintains the status of all incident resources. The Resources Unit plays a significant role in preparing the written Incident Action Plan.
- Situation Unit: Collects and analyzes information on the current situation, prepares situation displays and situation summaries, and develops maps and projections.
- Documentation Unit: Provides duplication services, including the written Incident Action Plan. Maintains and archives all incident-related documentation.
- Demobilization Unit: Assists in ensuring that resources are released from the incident in an orderly, safe, and cost-effective manner.

Planning Section

Visual 5.21

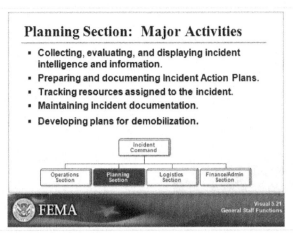

Instructor Notes: Present the following key points

The major activities of the Planning Section may include:

- Collecting, evaluating, and displaying incident intelligence and information.
- Preparing and documenting Incident Action Plans.
- Tracking resources assigned to the incident.
- Maintaining incident documentation.
- Developing plans for demobilization.

Visual 5.22

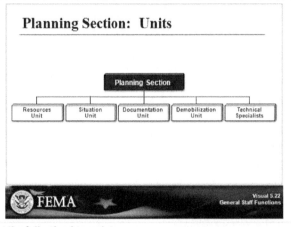

Instructor Notes: Present the following key points

The Planning Section can be further staffed with four Units. In addition, Technical Specialists who provide special expertise useful in incident management and response may also be assigned to work in the Planning Section. Depending on the needs, Technical Specialists may also be assigned to other Sections in the organization.

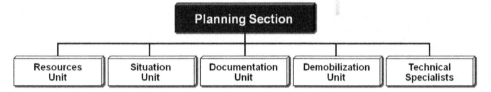

- Resources Unit: Conducts all check-in activities and maintains the status of all incident resources. The Resources Unit plays a significant role in preparing the written Incident Action Plan.
- Situation Unit: Collects and analyzes information on the current situation, prepares situation displays and situation summaries, and develops maps and projections.
- Documentation Unit: Provides duplication services, including the written Incident Action Plan. Maintains and archives all incident-related documentation.
- Demobilization Unit: Assists in ensuring that resources are released from the incident in an orderly, safe, and cost-effective manner.

Visual 5.23

> ## Activity: Planning Section Units
>
> <u>Instructions</u>: Working individually . . .
> 1. Review the Planning Section chart in your Student Manual.
> 2. Determine which of the Units would:
>   - Maintain a record of actions taken during an incident.
>   - Provide a map of the incident area.
>   - Oversee check-in procedures.
> 3. Be prepared to share your answers in 5 minutes.
>
> FEMA   Visual 5.23
> General Staff Functions

Instructor Notes: Present the following key points

Activity Purpose: To reinforce the participants' understanding of the Planning Section Units.

Instructions: Working individually:

1. Review the Planning Section chart in your Student Manual.
2. Determine which of the Units would:
    - Maintain a record of actions taken during an incident.
    - Provide a map of the incident area.
    - Oversee check-in procedures.
3. Be prepared to share your answers in 5 minutes.

Time: 10 minutes

Debrief Instructions:

1. Monitor the time. Notify the participants when 2 minutes remain.
2. Ask for volunteers to present their group's answers.

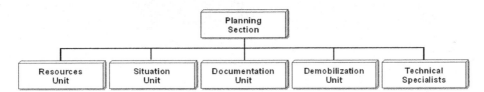

Which Planning Section Unit would maintain a record of actions taken during an incident?

Acknowledge the participants' responses. If not mentioned, tell the participants that the correct answer is the Documentation Unit. The Documentation Unit maintains and archives documentation on incident actions.

If you needed a map of the incident area, which Planning Section Unit would you go to?

Acknowledge the participants' responses. If not mentioned, tell the participants that the correct answer is the Situation Unit. The Situation Unit develops maps and projections and prepares situation displays and situation summaries.

If you needed to check in at an incident, which Planning Section Unit would you go to?

Acknowledge the participants' responses. If not mentioned, tell the participants that the correct answer is the Resources Unit. The Resources Unit conducts all check-in activities and maintains the status of all incident resources.

Logistics Section

Visual 5.24

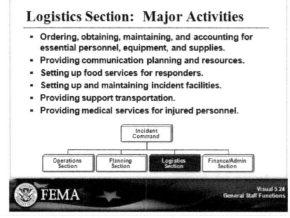

Instructor Notes: Present the following key points

The Logistics Section is responsible for all of the services and support needs, including:

- Ordering, obtaining, maintaining, and accounting for essential personnel, equipment, and supplies.
- Providing communication planning and resources.
- Setting up food services for responders.
- Setting up and maintaining incident facilities.
- Providing support transportation.
- Providing medical services to incident personnel.

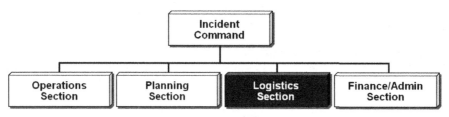

Visual 5.25

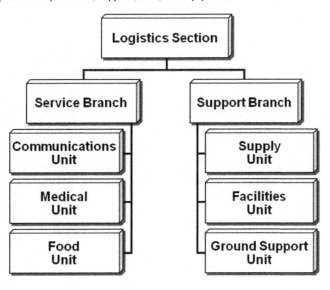

Instructor Notes: Present the following key points

The Logistics Section can be further staffed by two Branches and six Units. Remember that the Logistics Section provides support incident personnel only.

The titles of the Units are descriptive of their responsibilities.

Service Branch

The Logistics Service Branch can be staffed to include a:

- Communications Unit: Prepares and implements the Incident Communications Plan (ICS-205), distributes and maintains communications equipment, supervises the Incident Communications Center, and establishes adequate communications over the incident.
- Medical Unit: Develops the Medical Plan (ICS-206), provides first aid and light medical treatment for personnel assigned to the incident, and prepares procedures for a major medical emergency.
- Food Unit: Supplies the food and potable water for all incident facilities and personnel, and obtains the necessary equipment and supplies to operate food service facilities at Bases and Camps.

Support Branch

The Logistics Support Branch can be staffed to include a:

- Supply Unit: Determines the type and amount of supplies needed to support the incident. The Unit orders, receives, stores, and distributes supplies, services, and nonexpendable equipment. All resource orders are placed through the Supply Unit. The Unit maintains inventory and accountability of supplies and equipment.
- Facilities Unit: Sets up and maintains required facilities to support the incident. Provides managers for the Incident Base and Camps. Also responsible for facility security and facility maintenance services such as sanitation, lighting, and cleanup.
- Ground Support Unit: Prepares the Transportation Plan. Arranges for, activates, and documents the fueling, maintenance, and repair of ground resources. Arranges for the transportation of personnel, supplies, food, and equipment.

Finance and Administration Section

Visual 5.26

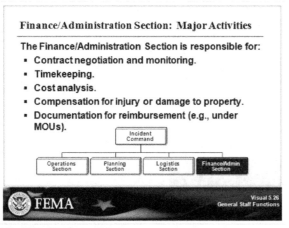

Instructor Notes: Present the following key points

The Finance/Administration Section is set up for any incident that requires incident-specific financial management. The Finance/Administration Section is responsible for:

- Contract negotiation and monitoring
- Timekeeping
- Cost analysis
- Compensation for injury or damage to property
- Documentation for reimbursement (e.g., under memorandums of understanding (MOUs)

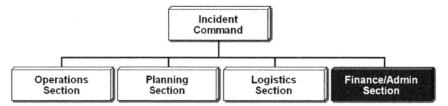

Visual 5.27

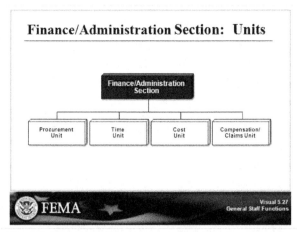

Instructor Notes: Present the following key points

The Finance/Administration Section can be further staffed with four Units.

- Procurement Unit: Responsible for administering all financial matters pertaining to vendor contracts, leases, and fiscal agreements.
- Time Unit: Responsible for incident personnel time recording.
- Cost Unit: Collects all cost data, performs cost effectiveness analyses, provides cost estimates, and makes cost savings recommendations.
- Compensation/Claims Unit: Responsible for the overall management and direction of all administrative matters pertaining to compensation for injury-related and claims-related activities kept for the incident.

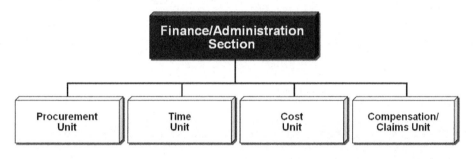

Activity: Section Chiefs

Visual 5.28

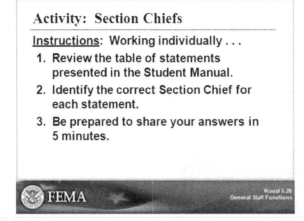

Activity: Section Chiefs

Instructions: Working individually . . .

1. Review the table of statements presented in the Student Manual.
2. Identify the correct Section Chief for each statement.
3. Be prepared to share your answers in 5 minutes.

FEMA

Visual 5.28
General Staff Functions

Instructor Notes: Present the following key points

Activity Purpose: To review the General Staff Section responsibilities.

Instructions: Working individually:

1. Review the table in your Student Manual.
2. Identify the correct Section Chief for each statement.
3. Be prepared to share your answers in 5 minutes.

Time: 10 minutes

Debrief Instructions:

1. Monitor the time. Notify the participants when 2 minutes remain.
2. Ask for volunteers to present their answers.

	Statement	Which Section Chief?
1	In advance of severe flooding, there is a need to get generators and communications equipment to the Staging Areas to equip advance response teams. My Section is responsible for making sure the needed equipment arrives at the Staging Areas.	
2	As the response is underway, my Section tracks all personnel participating in the response.	
3	My Section conducts response activities such as search and rescue, and first aid services being provided to disaster survivors.	
4	I support the incident response activities by overseeing contracting for needed supplies and services that are not already available.	

Acknowledge the participants' responses. Ask for volunteers to identify the correct Section Chief for each statement. If not mentioned, tell the participants that the correct answers are:

1. Logistics Section Chief
2. Planning Section Chief
3. Operations Section Chief
4. Finance/Administration Section Chief

Activity: General Staff Functions

Visual 5.29

Instructor Notes: Present the following key points

Activity Purpose: To reinforce participants' understanding of General Staff functions.

Instructions: Working in groups:

1. Review the scenario presented in your Student Manual.
2. Use what you've learned to answer the questions for each part of the activity before proceeding to the next page. Write your answers on chart paper.
3. When you've answered each set of questions, move on to the next page.
4. Select a spokesperson and be prepared to discuss your answers to all the questions in 15 minutes.

Time: 20 minutes

Scenario Part 1: A store employee at a small shopping mall discovers a package leaking a noxious smelling chemical in a storage room. No one is sure how long the box has been there, or how long it has been leaking. Employees and customers are beginning to complain about feeling lightheaded and nauseous. The business owner calls 911. In the meantime, the mall security manager arrives to see why people are rushing out of the store. The security manager establishes the initial ICS organization.

Question:

- In the ICS organization described above, the mall security manager has assumed which role?

Scenario Part 2: A Battalion Chief and hazmat team arrive at the scene. In addition, a law enforcement patrol car with one officer has arrived to help with perimeter control.

Questions:

- What must happen before the HazMat Battalion Chief assumes the Incident Commander role?
- What role might the police officer play in the ICS organization?

Scenario Part 3: A transfer of command occurs and the HazMat Battalion Chief assumes the Incident Commander role. The Command and General Staff positions are filled as shown on the chart.

Questions:

- Does the Incident Commander have a manageable span of control?
- What is the title of the person in charge of the Perimeter Security Strike Team?
- What member of the Command Staff would go in the box with the question mark?

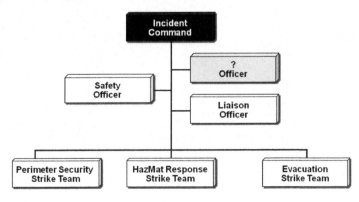

Caption: Organization chart with Incident Commander, Safety Officer, [?] Officer, Liaison Officer, Perimeter Security Strike Team, HazMat Response Strike Team, and Evacuation Strike Team.

Scenario Part 4: To maintain span of control as the incident expands, the Incident Commander establishes an Operations Section.

Questions:

- What is the role of the Operations Section?
- What is the ICS title of the person in charge of the Operations Section?

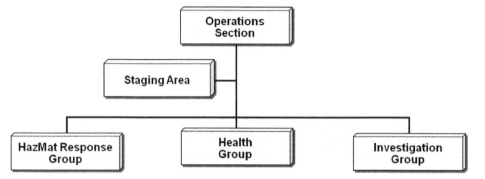

Caption: Organization chart showing the Operations Section. Reporting to the Operations Section are the following: Staging Area, HazMat Response Group, Health Group, and Investigation Group.

Scenario Part 5: After the first hour, the Incident Commander establishes a second Section that will develop the Incident Action Plan and track the status of resources on the scene.

Question:

- What is the correct title of this Section?

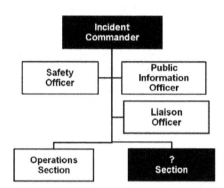

Caption: Organization chart with Incident Commander, Command Staff, and Operations Section. A second Section has been added.

Scenario Part 6: In an interview, the business owner mentions that she has received threats from a recently terminated employee. The substance has yet to be identified. Given these circumstances, there is a need to find witnesses and locate people who may have come in contact with the package. Interview areas have been set up in the mall parking lot. There are an increasing number of response personnel at the scene, creating the need for communications support along with food and drinks.

Question:

- Which Section is responsible for providing these support resources?

Scenario Part 7: Cleanup is complete, and the few exposed customers and staff have been located and are undergoing treatment. The operation is now shifting to an ongoing investigation of the disgruntled former employee.

Question:

- Which resources would you demobilize?

Debrief Instructions:

1. Monitor the time. Notify the participants when 5 minutes remain.
2. After 15 minutes have passed, ask the groups to present their answers.
3. If not mentioned by participants, provide the following correct answers:

In the ICS organization described above, the faculty member has assumed which role? The Incident Commander. The mall security manager was the first on the scene and was responsible for establishing the initial ICS organization. He or she was functioning as the Incident Commander.

What must happen before the HazMat Battalion Chief assumes the Incident Commander role? There must be a transfer of command briefing for the incoming Incident Commander. In this case, the Battalion Chief must be briefed by the mall security manager.

What role might the police officer play in the ICS organization? The police officer is a single resource in the ICS organization.

Does the Incident Commander have a manageable span of control? The Incident Commander does have a manageable span of control.

What is the title of the person in charge of the Perimeter Security Strike Team? A Leader would be in charge of the Perimeter Security Strike Team.

What member of the Command Staff would go in the box with the question mark? The Public Information Officer is the other member of the Command Staff.

What is the role of the Operations Section? The Operations Section directs and controls all tactical operations for the incident.

What is the ICS title of the person in charge of the Operations Section? The correct title of the person in charge of the Operations Section is "Chief."

What is the correct title of this Section? If not mentioned, tell the participants that the correct answer is the Planning Section. As part of its many responsibilities, the Planning Section prepares and documents the Incident Action Plan (IAP).

Which Section is responsible for providing these support resources? If not mentioned, tell the participants that the correct answer is the Logistics Section. As part of its responsibilities, the Logistics Section is responsible for all services and support needs, such as food and medical services for responders.

Which resources would you demobilize?

Although there is no single correct answer, it would most likely be the hazmat response resources. Use this activity as an opportunity to have the participants think about the need for demobilization planning. Some of the factors that should be considered during the demobilization of this incident include continued need for investigative resources, continued media coverage, etc.

Unit Summary

Visual 5.30

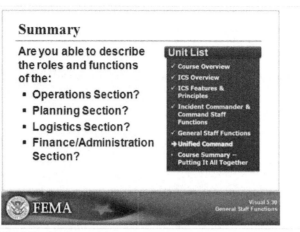

Instructor Notes: Present the following key points

Are you able to describe the roles and functions of the:

- Operations Section?
- Planning Section?
- Logistics Section?
- Finance/Administration Section?

Ask if anyone has any questions about anything covered in this unit.

The next unit will focus on the features and organizational structures related to Unified Command.

UNIT 6: UNIFIED COMMAND

This page intentionally left blank

IS-0100b – Introduction to Incident Command System (ICS) Instructor Guide

Unit Objectives

At the end of this unit, the participants should be able to:

- Define Unified Command.
- List the advantages of Unified Command.
- Identify the primary features of Unified Command.
- Differentiate between command and coordination.

Scope

- Unit Introduction
- Unified Command
- Unified Command: Benefits
- Unified Command: Features
- Unified Command: Organization
- Unified Command: Strategies
- Coordination
- Unit Summary

Methodology

The instructors will review the objectives for this unit and then provide an overview of Unified Command. An activity involving a hazardous material spill will be used to illustrate the benefits of Unified Command.

Next the instructors will present the benefits, features, and organizational structures related to Unified Command. The instructors will discuss incident coordination and the Joint Information Center, or JIC. Participants will then work in teams to apply Unified Command principles in an activity. Two quick-reference guides are included in this unit—ICS Organization and Position Titles—that participants can use on the job.

The instructors will then transition to the next unit, which focuses on putting together the information learned in this course to prepare to implement ICS.

Materials

- PowerPoint visuals 6.1 – 6.13
- Instructor Guide
- PowerPoint slides and a computer display system
- Student Manual

Time Plan

A suggested time plan for this unit is shown below. More or less time may be required, based on the experience level of the group.

Topic	Time
Unit Introduction	5 minutes
Activity: Optimal Strategy	10 minutes
Unified Command: Definition and Benefits	5 minutes
Unified Command: Features	2 minutes
Unified Command: Organization	5 minutes
Unified Command: Strategies	5 minutes
Coordination	5 minutes
Activity: Unified Command	25 minutes
Unit Summary	3 minutes
Total Time	**1 hours, 5 minutes**

Unit Introduction

Visual 6.1

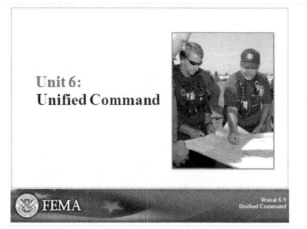

Instructor Notes: Present the following key points

The previous units covered the Incident Command Systems (ICS) fundamentals. This unit introduces you to a more advanced concept, called Unified Command.

Unified Command:

- Applies ICS in incidents involving multiple jurisdictions or agencies.
- Enables institutions and agencies with different legal, geographic, and functional responsibilities to coordinate, plan, and interact effectively.

Visual 6.2

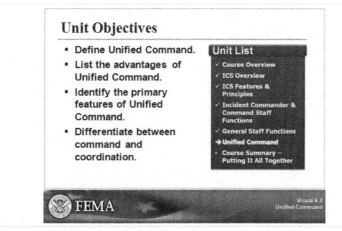

Instructor Notes: Present the following key points

By the end of this unit, you should be able to:

- Define Unified Command.
- List the advantages of Unified Command.
- Identify the primary features of Unified Command.
- Differentiate between command and coordination.

Visual 6.3

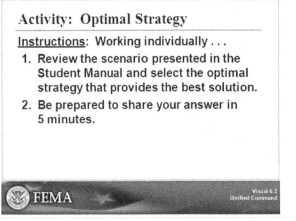

Activity: Optimal Strategy

Instructions: Working individually . . .

1. Review the scenario presented in the Student Manual and select the optimal strategy that provides the best solution.
2. Be prepared to share your answer in 5 minutes.

FEMA

Visual 6.3
Unified Command

Instructor Notes: Present the following key points

Activity Purpose: To reinforce participants' understanding of the importance of Unified Command.

Instructions: Working individually:

1. Read the scenario below and select the optimal strategy that provides the best solution.
2. Be prepared to share your answer in 5 minutes.

Time: 10 minutes

Debrief Instructions:

1. Monitor the time. Notify the participants when 2 minutes remain.
2. Ask for volunteers to present their answers.

Scenario: Response to a hazardous materials spill involves hazmat cleanup crews, law enforcement agencies to conduct evacuations and perimeter control, and public works responders to help with cleanup and rerouting traffic.

Select the optimal strategy:

- Divide the incident along functional lines so that each agency can establish its own ICS organization with well-defined areas of responsibilities.
- Create a single ICS incident structure that allows for an effective multiagency approach.
- Allow the participants time to select a strategy. Facilitate a discussion. If not mentioned by the participants, make the following points:
    - o Unified Command: The preferred solution is to create a single ICS incident structure with a built-in process for an effective and responsible multijurisdictional or multiagency approach. This solution became Unified Command.
    - o Separate Commands: The other option of dividing the incident into separate command structures may be the simplest political solution but is often not effective. If separate commands are used, there is a danger of:
        - ▪ Critical life-safety incident objectives being missed because each command assumes that another one was taking responsibility.
        - ▪ Duplication of efforts and competing for the same scarce resources.
        - ▪ Inconsistent messages being reported to the media and community.

Unified Command: Definition and Benefits

Visual 6.4

Unified Command

The Unified Command organization consists of the Incident Commanders from the various jurisdictions or organizations operating together to form a single command structure.

Fire & Rescue Incident Commander

Local Law Enforcement Incident Commander

HazMat Incident Commander

FEMA

Visual 6.4
Unified Command

Instructor Notes: Present the following key points

Unified Command:

- Applies ICS in incidents involving multiple jurisdictions or organizations.
- Enables institutions and agencies with different legal, geographic, and functional responsibilities to coordinate, plan, and interact effectively.

The Incident Commanders within the Unified Command make joint decisions and speak as one voice. Any differences are worked out within the Unified Command.

Unity of command is maintained. Each responder reports to a single supervisor within his or her area of expertise. Within a Unified Command, the police officer would not tell the firefighters how to do their job.

Visual 6.5

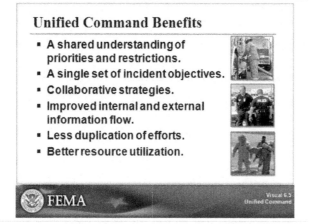

Instructor Notes: Present the following key points

In a Unified Command, institutions and responding agencies blend into an integrated, unified team. A unified approach results in:

- A shared understanding of priorities and restrictions.
- A single set of incident objectives.
- Collaborative strategies.
- Improved internal and external information flow.
- Less duplication of efforts
- Better resource utilization.

Unified Command: Features

Visual 6.6

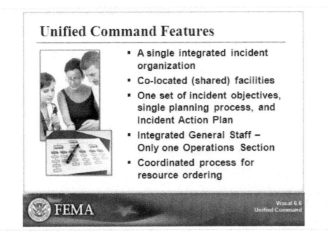

Instructor Notes: Present the following key points

Review the following features of Unified Command:

- A Single Integrated Incident Organization: As a team effort, Unified Command overcomes much of the inefficiency and duplication of effort that can occur when agencies from different functional and geographic jurisdictions, or agencies at different levels of government, operate without a common system or organizational framework.
- Co-located (Shared) Facilities: In a Unified Command, incident facilities are co-located or shared. There is one single Incident Command Post.
- One Set of Incident Objectives, Single Planning Process, and Incident Action Plan: Unified Command uses one set of incident objectives and a single planning process, and produces one Incident Action Plan (IAP). The planning process for Unified Command is similar to the process used on single-jurisdiction incidents.
- Integrated General Staff: Integrating multijurisdictional and/or multiagency personnel into various other functional areas may be beneficial. For example:
  - In Operations and Planning, Deputy Section Chiefs can be designated from an adjacent jurisdiction.
  - In Logistics, a Deputy Logistics Section Chief from another agency or jurisdiction can help to coordinate incident support.

Incident Commanders within the Unified Command must concur on the selection of the General Staff Section Chiefs. The Operations Section Chief must have full authority to implement the tactics within the Incident Action Plan.

- Coordinated Process for Resource Ordering: The Incident Commanders within the Unified Command work together to establish resource ordering procedures that allow for:
  - Deployment of scarce resources to meet high-priority objectives.
  - Potential cost savings through agreements on cost sharing for essential services.

Unified Command: Organization

Visual 6.7

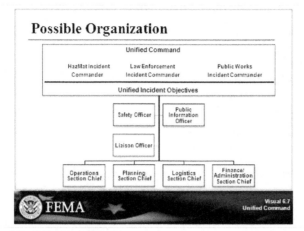

Instructor Notes: Present the following key points

Review the possible Unified Command organizational structure for a hazardous materials incident provided on the visual.

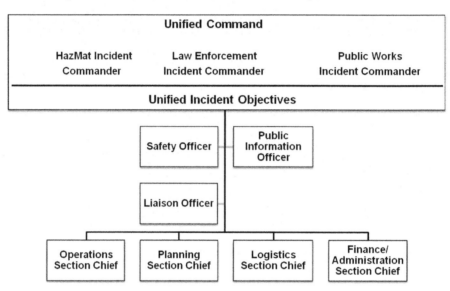

Visual 6.8

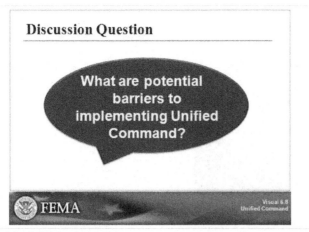

Instructor Notes: Present the following key points

Ask the participants: What are some potential barriers to implementing Unified Command?

Then follow up by asking the participants: How can you overcome these barriers?

Acknowledge the participants' responses. Proceed to the next slide for a discussion of ways to overcome barriers and make Unified Command work.

Unified Command: Strategies

Visual 6.9

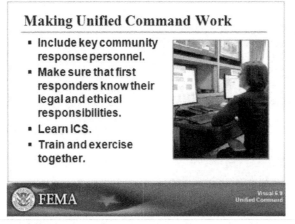

Instructor Notes: Present the following key points

For Unified Command to be used successfully, it is important that institutions and agencies prepare by:

- Including key community response personnel in your institution's planning process.
- Making sure that first responders know what the institution's legal and ethical responsibilities are during an event.
- Learning ICS so that they can blend into the response structure.
- Train and exercise together.

Coordination

Visual 6.10

Instructor Notes: Present the following key points

Coordination includes the activities that ensure that the onsite ICS organization receives the information, resources, and support needed to achieve the incident objectives. Coordination takes place in a number of entities and at all levels of government.

Examples of coordination activities include:

- Establishing policy based on interactions with agency executives, other agencies, and stakeholders.
- Collecting, analyzing, and disseminating information to support the establishment of a common operating picture.
- Establishing priorities among incidents.
- Resolving critical resource issues.
- Facilitating logistics support and resource tracking.
- Synchronizing public information messages to ensure everyone is speaking with one voice.

Visual 6.11

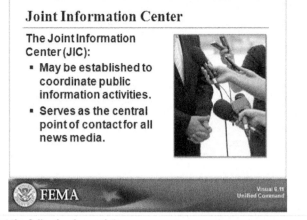

Instructor Notes: Present the following key points

As mentioned previously, an Emergency Operations Center (EOC) can serve as a coordination entity. Another coordination entity is the Joint Information Center (JIC). The JIC:

- May be established to coordinate all incident-related public information activities.
- Serves as the central point of contact for all news media. When possible, public information officials from all participating agencies should co-locate at the JIC.

JICs may be established at various levels of government or at incident sites.

Activity

Visual 6.12

Activity: Unified Command

Instructions: Working as a team . . .

1. Review the scenario and questions presented in the Student Manual.
2. Refer to the quick-reference guides in the Student Manual as needed.
3. Select a spokesperson and be prepared to present your work in 20 minutes.

FEMA

Visual 6.12
Unified Command

Instructor Notes: Present the following key points

Activity Purpose: To reinforce participants' understanding of the Unified Command structure.

Instructions: Working as a team:

1. Review the scenario and questions presented in the Student Manual.
2. Refer to the quick-reference guides in the Student Manual as needed.
3. Select a spokesperson and be prepared to share your answers in 20 minutes.

Time: 25 minutes

Debrief Instructions:

1. Monitor the time. Notify the participants when 5 minutes remain.
2. Ask one team to present who they would include in the Unified Command structure.
3. Ask the other teams if they had different responses. Compare the similarities and differences among the teams. There is no one correct answer.
4. Next, ask a different team to present their answer to the next question. After the team presents, ask the other teams to comment. Continue with this process until all teams have presented.
5. Summarize the key learning points. Make sure to provide any needed guidance or correct any misunderstandings or inaccurate application of ICS principles and concepts.

Scenario: A football team is returning home from a State tournament. Their bus is involved in an accident on the bridge that marks the county line.

- Most of the bus is in Franklin County.
- A small part of the bus is in Revere County (their home county).

Questions:

- Which agencies/organizations should be included in the Unified Command structure?
- Which ICS positions/Sections will be activated?
- How many Operations Section Chiefs will be assigned representing each of the agencies?
- What is one example of an incident objective that the Unified Command group might establish?

Unit Summary

Visual 6.13

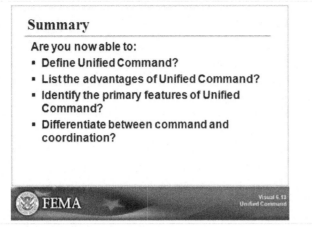

Instructor Notes: Present the following key points

Are you now able to:

- Define Unified Command?
- List the advantages of Unified Command?
- Identify the primary features of Unified Command?
- Differentiate between command and coordination?

The purpose of this unit was to familiarize you with Unified Command features. Additional ICS training is required to prepare you to implement Unified Command. Remember that Unified Command:

- Applies ICS in incidents involving multiple jurisdictions or agencies.
- Enables institutions and agencies with different legal, geographic, and functional responsibilities to coordinate, plan, and interact effectively.

Ask if anyone has any questions about anything covered in this unit.

The next unit focuses on putting together the information learned in this course to prepare to implement ICS.

UNIT 7: COURSE SUMMARY – PUTTING IT ALL TOGETHER

This page intentionally left blank

Unit Objectives

At the end of this unit, the participants should be able to:

- Describe the steps to take to ensure you are ready to assume ICS responsibilities.
- Assess your organization's readiness for implementing ICS.
- Take the final exam.

Scope

- Unit Introduction
- Assuming Accountability
- Dispatch/Deployment and Check-in
- Recordkeeping
- Lengthy Assignments
- Demobilization
- Plans, Policies, and Regulations
- Training, Credentialing, and Exercising
- Making ICS Work
- Additional Resources
- Final Exam
- Course Evaluation

Methodology

The final unit begins with emphasis on the personal actions that each person must take to make ICS work. The unit then covers recordkeeping and demobilization. Next, the instructors will discuss how to assess an institution's preparedness for implementing ICS. The instructors will then provide instructions on taking the final exam. To conclude the unit, the instructors will emphasize to the group the importance of providing course feedback.

Materials

- PowerPoint visuals 7.1 – 7.12
- Instructor Guide
- PowerPoint slides and a computer display system
- Student Manual

Time Plan

A suggested time plan for this unit is shown below. More or less time may be required, based on the experience level of the group.

Topic	Time
Unit Introduction	5 minutes
Assuming Accountability	5 minutes
Dispatch/Deployment and Check-in	5 minutes
Recordkeeping	5 minutes
Lengthy Assignments	5 minutes
Demobilization	5 minutes
Plans, Policies, and Regulations	10 minutes
Training, Credentialing, and Exercising	5 minutes
Making ICS Work	5 minutes
Additional Resources	5 minutes
Final Exam	30 minutes
Course Evaluation	5 minutes
Total Time	**1 hours, 30 minutes**

Unit Introduction

Visual 7.1

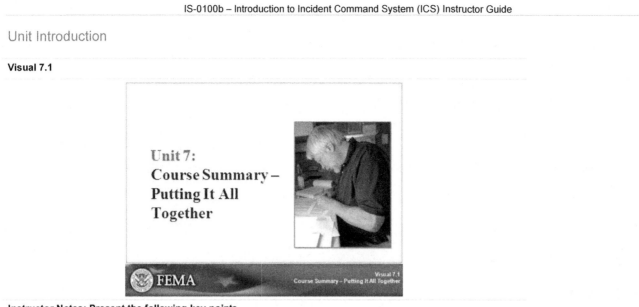

Instructor Notes: Present the following key points

You should now be familiar with the core system features of ICS and the ICS organizational roles and responsibilities.

"Putting it all together" means that:

- You are personally ready to follow the ICS principles.
- Your organization is ready to implement ICS.

Visual 7.2

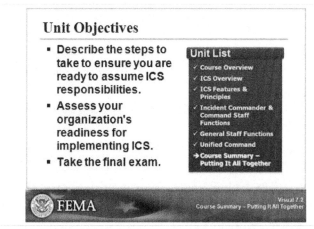

Instructor Notes: Present the following key points

By the end of this unit, you should be able to:

- Describe the steps to take to ensure you are ready to assume ICS responsibilities.
- Assess your organization's readiness for implementing ICS.
- Take the final exam.

Assuming Accountability

Visual 7.3

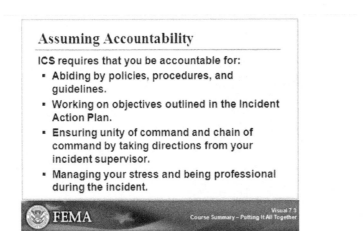

Instructor Notes: Present the following key points

ICS requires that you be accountable for:

- Abiding by policies, procedures, and guidelines.
- Working on objectives outlined in the Incident Action Plan.
- Ensuring unity of command and chain of command by taking directions from your incident supervisor.
- Managing your stress and being professional during the incident.

Ask the participants: Are you ready to assume accountability?

Dispatch/Deployment and Check-In

Visual 7.4

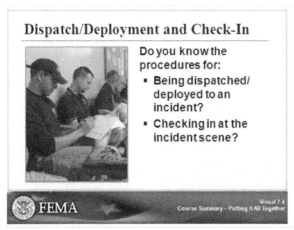

Instructor Notes: Present the following key points

When an incident occurs, you must be mobilized or assigned to become part of the incident response. In other words, until you are mobilized to the incident organization, you remain in your everyday role.

After being mobilized, your first task is to check in and receive an assignment.

Ask the participants: Do you know the procedure for being dispatched/deployed to an incident? Do you know the procedure for check-in?

Visual 7.5

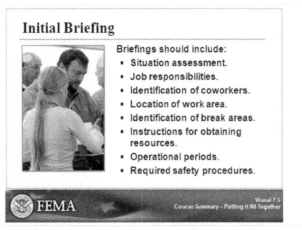

Initial Briefing

Briefings should include:
- Situation assessment.
- Job responsibilities.
- Identification of coworkers.
- Location of work area.
- Identification of break areas.
- Instructions for obtaining resources.
- Operational periods.
- Required safety procedures.

FEMA

Visual 7.5
Course Summary – Putting It All Together

Instructor Notes: Present the following key points

After check-in, you will locate your incident supervisor and obtain your initial briefing. The briefings you receive and give should include:

- Current assessment of the situation.
- Identification of your specific job responsibilities.
- Identification of coworkers.
- Location of work area.
- Identification of break areas, as appropriate.
- Procedural instructions for obtaining needed resources.
- Operational periods/work shifts.
- Required safety procedures and personal protective equipment (PPE), as appropriate.

Ask the participants: Do you have a checklist to help ensure that you receive all needed information?

Recordkeeping

Visual 7.6

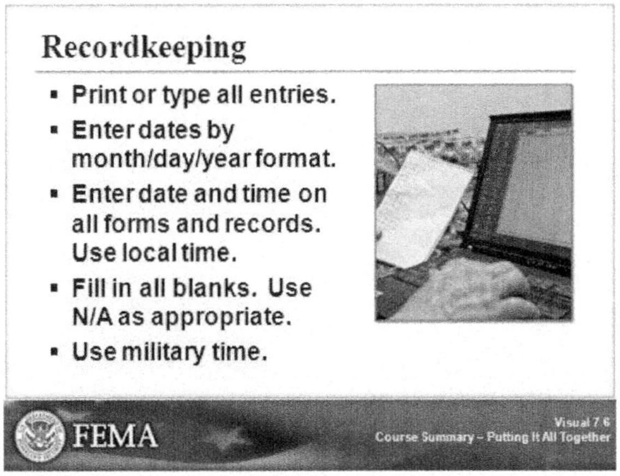

Instructor Notes: Present the following key points

All incidents require some form of recordkeeping. Requirements vary depending upon the agencies involved and the nature of the incident. Below are general guidelines for incident recordkeeping:

- Print or type all entries.
- Enter dates by month/day/year format.
- Enter date and time on all forms and records. Use local time.
- Fill in all blanks. Use N/A as appropriate.
- Use military 24-hour time.

Lengthy Assignments

Visual 7.7

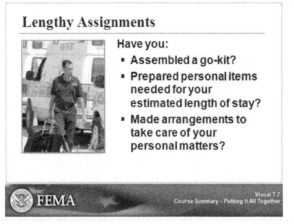

Instructor Notes: Present the following key points

Many incidents last only a short time. However, if you were asked to deploy to support a lengthy assignment away from home, you would need to prepare yourself and your family.

Ask the participants if they have:

- Assembled a travel or go-kit containing any special technical information (e.g., maps, manuals, contact lists, and reference materials).
- Prepared personal items needed for your estimated length of stay, including medications, cash, credit cards.
- Made arrangements to take care of your personal and home matters.

Demobilization

Visual 7.8

Demobilization

At the end of your assignment:

- Complete all tasks and required forms/reports.
- Brief replacements, subordinates, and supervisor.
- Evaluate the performance of subordinates.
- Follow check-out procedures.
- Return any incident-issued equipment or other nonexpendable supplies.
- Complete post-incident reports, critiques, evaluations, and medical followup.
- Complete all time records or other accounting obligations.

FEMA   Visual 7.8
                          Course Summary – Putting It All Together

Instructor Notes: Present the following key points

Resource demobilization occurs at the end of your assignment or when the incident is resolved. Before leaving an incident assignment, you should:

- Complete all tasks and required forms/reports.
- Brief replacements, subordinates, and supervisor.
- Evaluate the performance of subordinates.
- Follow check-out procedures.
- Return any incident-issued equipment or other nonexpendable supplies.
- Complete post-incident reports, critiques, evaluations, and medical follow-up.
- Complete all time records or other accounting obligations.

Making ICS Work

Visual 7.9

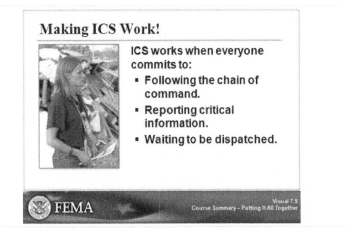

Instructor Notes: Present the following key points

Using ICS at incidents succeeds when everyone assumes personal accountability by:

- Not going around the chain of command. Only take direction from your immediate ICS supervisor (might not be your day-to-day supervisor). Exchange of information is encouraged; however, all assignments and resource requests must go through your immediate ICS supervisor.
- Reporting critical information about safety hazards, status, changing conditions/needs within assigned areas, and resource needs.
- Not self-dispatching. Do not start responding unless you are deployed or your actions are critical for life and safety. Make sure to check in when you begin your assignment. If the plan is not working or your assigned activity cannot be completed, tell your supervisor. Do not create your own plan of action.

Additional Resources

Visual 7.10

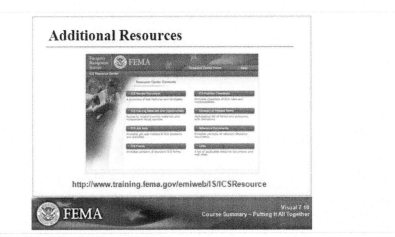

Instructor Notes: Present the following key points

Additional resources can be found at the EMI online ICS Resource Center. The Resource Center can be accessed at http://www.training.fema.gov/emiweb/IS/ICSResource.

Ask if anyone has any questions before continuing to the course exam.

Final Exam

Visual 7.11

Instructor Notes: Present the following key points

Present the following IS-0100.b test instructions:

Instructions:

1. Take a few moments to review your Student Manual and identify any questions.
2. Make sure that you get all of your questions answered prior to beginning the final test.
3. When taking the test...
   - Read each item carefully.
   - Circle your answer on the test.
   - Check your work and take the test online.

Tell the participants that they may refer to their Student Manuals and the NIMS document when completing this test. When the review is completed, distribute the exams. Remain in the room to monitor the exam and to be available for questions. Collect the completed exams.

Instructor Note: To receive a certificate of completion, participants must take the 10-question multiple-choice posttestand score 75 percent on the test.

- Participants submit their tests online, and upon successful completion receive an e-mail message with a link to their electronic certification.
  - Go to http://training.fema.gov/IS/crslist.asp and click on the link for IS-0100.b.
  - Click on "Take Final Exam."

Course Evaluation

Visual 7.12

Instructor Notes: Present the following key points

Completing the course evaluation form is important. Your comments will be used to evaluate the effectiveness of this course and make changes for future versions.

Please use the course evaluation forms provided by the organization sponsoring the course.

GLOSSARY

Agency: A division of government with a specific function offering a particular kind of assistance. In the Incident Command System, agencies are defined either as jurisdictional (having statutory responsibility for incident management) or as assisting or cooperating (providing resources or other assistance). Governmental organizations are most often in charge of an incident, though in certain circumstances private sector organizations may be included. Additionally, nongovernmental organizations may be included to provide support.

Agency Administrator or Executive: The official responsible for administering policy for an agency or jurisdiction. An Agency Administrator/Executive (or other public official with jurisdictional responsibility for the incident) usually makes the decision to establish an Area Command.

Agency Dispatch: The agency or jurisdictional facility from which resources are sent to incidents.

Agency Representative: A person assigned by a primary, assisting, or cooperating Federal, State, tribal, or local government agency or private organization that has been delegated authority to make decisions affecting that agency's or organization's participation in incident management activities following appropriate consultation with the leadership of that agency.

All-Hazards: Describing an incident, natural or manmade, that warrants action to protect life, property, environment, public health or safety, and minimize disruptions of government, social, or economic activities.

Allocated Resource: Resource dispatched to an incident.

Area Command: An organization established to oversee the management of multiple incidents that are each being handled by a separate Incident Command System organization or to oversee the management of a very large or evolving incident that has multiple incident management teams engaged. An agency administrator/executive or other public official with jurisdictional responsibility for the incident usually makes the decision to establish an Area Command. An Area Command is activated only if necessary, depending on the complexity of the incident and incident management span-of-control considerations.

Assessment: The process of acquiring, collecting, processing, examining, analyzing, evaluating, monitoring, and interpreting the data, information, evidence, objects, measurements, images, sound, etc., whether tangible or intangible, to provide a basis for decision-making.

Assigned Resource: Resource checked in and assigned work tasks on an incident.

Assignment: Task given to a personnel resource to perform within a given operational period that is based on operational objectives defined in the Incident Action Plan.

Assistant: Title for subordinates of the Command Staff positions. The title indicates a level of technical capability, qualifications, and responsibility subordinate to the primary positions. Assistants may also be assigned to Unit Leaders.

Assisting Agency: An agency or organization providing personnel, services, or other resources to the agency with direct responsibility for incident management.

Available Resource: Resource assigned to an incident, checked in, and available for a mission assignment, normally located in a Staging Area.

Badging: The assignment of physical incident-specific credentials to establish legitimacy and limit access to various incident sites.

Branch: The organizational level having functional or geographical responsibility for major aspects of incident operations. A Branch is organizationally situated between the Section Chief and the Division or Group in the Operations Section, and between the Section and Units in the Logistics Section. Branches are identified by the use of Roman numerals or by functional area.

Cache: A predetermined complement of tools, equipment, and/or supplies stored in a designated location, available for incident use.

Camp: A geographical site, within the general incident area, separate from the Incident Base, equipped and staffed to provide sleeping, food, water, and sanitary services to incident personnel.

Certifying Personnel: The process of authoritatively attesting that individuals meet professional standards for the training, experience, and performance required for key incident management functions.

Chain of Command: The orderly line of authority within the ranks of the incident management organization.

Check-In: The process through which resources first report to an incident. All responders, regardless of agency affiliation, must report in to receive an assignment in accordance with the procedures established by the Incident Commander.

Chief: The Incident Command System title for individuals responsible for management of functional Sections: Operations, Planning, Logistics, Finance/Administration, and Intelligence/Investigations (if established as a separate Section).

Command: The act of directing, ordering, or controlling by virtue of explicit statutory, regulatory, or delegated authority.

Command Staff: The staff who report directly to the Incident Commander, including the Public Information Officer, Safety Officer, Liaison Officer, and other positions as required. They may have an assistant or assistants, as needed.

Common Operating Picture: An overview of an incident by all relevant parties that provides incident information enabling the Incident Commander/Unified Command and any supporting agencies and organizations to make effective, consistent, and timely decisions.

Common Terminology: Normally used words and phrases—avoiding the use of different words/phrases for same concepts—to ensure consistency and to allow diverse incident management and support organizations to work together across a wide variety of incident management functions and hazard scenarios.

Communications: The process of transmission of information through verbal, written, or symbolic means.

Communications/Dispatch Center: An agency or interagency dispatcher center, 911 call center, emergency control or command dispatch center, or any naming convention given to the facility and staff that handles emergency calls from the public and communication with emergency management/response personnel. The center can serve as a primary coordination and support element of the multiagency coordination system (MACS) for an incident until other elements of the MACS are formally established.

Complex: Two or more individual incidents located in the same general area and assigned to a single Incident Commander or to Unified Command.

Cooperating Agency: An agency supplying assistance other than direct operational or support functions or resources to the incident management effort.

Coordinate: To advance systematically an analysis and exchange of information among principals who have or may have a need to know certain information to carry out specific incident management responsibilities.

Corrective Actions: The implementation of procedures that are based on lessons learned from actual incidents or from training and exercises.

Credentialing: The authentication and verification of the certification and identity of designated incident managers and emergency responders.

Delegation of Authority: A statement provided to the Incident Commander by the agency executive delegating authority and assigning responsibility. The delegation of authority can include objectives, priorities, expectations, constraints, and other considerations or guidelines, as needed. Many agencies require written delegation of authority to be given to the Incident Commander prior to assuming command on larger incidents. Also known as Letter of Expectation.

Demobilization: The orderly, safe, and efficient return of an incident resource to its original location and status.

Deputy: A fully qualified individual who, in the absence of a superior, could be delegated the authority to manage a functional operation or perform a specific task. In some cases, a Deputy could act as relief for a superior and therefore must be fully qualified in the position. Deputies can be assigned to the Incident Commander, General Staff, and Branch Directors.

Director: The Incident Command System title for individuals responsible for supervision of a Branch.

Dispatch: The ordered movement of a resource or resources to an assigned operational mission, or an administrative move from one location to another.

Division: The organizational level having responsibility for operations within a defined geographic area. Divisions are established when the number of resources exceeds the manageable span of control of the Section Chief. See Group.

Emergency: Any incident, whether natural or manmade, that requires responsive action to protect life or property. Under the Robert T. Stafford Disaster Relief and Emergency Assistance Act, an emergency means any occasion or instance for which, in the determination of the President, Federal assistance is needed to supplement State and local efforts and capabilities to save lives and to protect property and public health and safety, or to lessen or avert the threat of a catastrophe in any part of the United States.

Emergency Management/Response Personnel: Includes Federal, State, territorial, tribal, substate regional, and local governments, private-sector organizations, critical infrastructure owners and operators, nongovernmental organizations, and all other organizations and individuals who assume an emergency management role. Also known as emergency responders.

Emergency Operations Center (EOC): The physical location at which the coordination of information and resources to support incident management (on-scene operations) activities normally takes place. An EOC may be a temporary facility or may be located in a more central or permanently established facility, perhaps at a higher level of organization within a jurisdiction. EOCs may be organized by major functional disciplines (e.g., fire, law enforcement, and medical services), by jurisdiction (e.g., Federal, State, regional, tribal, city, county), or some combination thereof.

Emergency Operations Plan (EOP): An ongoing plan for responding to a wide variety of potential hazards.

Emergency Public Information: Information that is disseminated primarily in anticipation of an emergency or during an emergency. In addition to providing situational information to the public, it also frequently provides directive actions required to be taken by the general public.

Evacuation: The organized, phased, and supervised withdrawal, dispersal, or removal of civilians from dangerous or potentially dangerous areas, and their reception and care in safe areas.

Event: See Planned Event.

External Affairs: Organizational element that provides accurate, coordinated, and timely information to affected audiences, including governments, media, the private sector, and the local populace.

Federal: Of or pertaining to the Federal Government of the United States of America.

Field Operations Guide: Durable pocket or desk guide that contains essential information required to perform specific assignments or functions.

Finance/Administration Section: The Incident Command System Section responsible for all administrative and financial considerations surrounding an incident.

Function: One of the five major activities in the Incident Command System: Command, Operations, Planning, Logistics, and Finance/Administration. A sixth function, Intelligence/Investigations, may be established, if required, to meet incident management needs. The term function is also used when describing the activity involved (e.g., the planning function).

General Staff: A group of incident management personnel organized according to function and reporting to the Incident Commander. The General Staff normally consists of the Operations Section Chief, Planning Section Chief, Logistics Section Chief, and Finance/Administration Section Chief. An Intelligence/Investigations Chief may be established, if required, to meet incident management needs.

Group: An organizational subdivision established to divide the incident management structure into functional areas of operation. Groups are composed of resources assembled to perform a special function not necessarily within a single geographic division. See Division.

Hazard: Something that is potentially dangerous or harmful, often the root cause of an unwanted outcome.

Identification and Authentication: For security purposes, process required for individuals and organizations that access the National Incident Management System information management system and, in particular, those that contribute information to the system (e.g., situation reports).

Incident: An occurrence or event, natural or manmade, that requires a response to protect life or property. Incidents can, for example, include major disasters, emergencies, terrorist attacks, terrorist threats, civil unrest, wildland and urban fires, floods, hazardous materials spills, nuclear accidents, aircraft accidents, earthquakes, hurricanes, tornadoes, tropical storms, tsunamis, war-related disasters, public health and medical emergencies, and other occurrences requiring an emergency response.

Incident Action Plan (IAP): An oral or written plan containing general objectives reflecting the overall strategy for managing an incident. It may include the identification of operational resources and assignments. It may also include attachments that provide direction and important information for management of the incident during one or more operational periods.

Incident Base: The location at which primary Logistics functions for an incident are coordinated and administered. There is only one Base per incident. (Incident name or other designator will be added to the term Base.) The Incident Command Post may be co-located with the Incident Base.

Incident Command: The Incident Command System organizational element responsible for overall management of the incident and consisting of the Incident Commander (either single or unified command structure) and any assigned supporting staff.

Incident Commander (IC): The individual responsible for all incident activities, including the development of strategies and tactics and the ordering and the release of resources. The IC has overall authority and responsibility for conducting incident operations and is responsible for the management of all incident operations at the incident site.

Incident Command Post (ICP): The field location where the primary functions are performed. The ICP may be co-located with the Incident Base or other incident facilities.

Incident Command System (ICS): A standardized on-scene emergency management construct specifically designed to provide for the adoption of an integrated organizational structure that reflects the complexity and demands of single or multiple incidents, without being hindered by jurisdictional boundaries. ICS is the combination of facilities, equipment, personnel, procedures, and communications operating within a common organizational structure, designed to aid in the management of resources during incidents. It is used for all kinds of emergencies and is applicable to small as well as large and complex incidents. ICS is used by various jurisdictions and functional agencies, both public and private, to organize field-level incident management operations.

Incident Management: The broad spectrum of activities and organizations providing effective and efficient operations, coordination, and support applied at all levels of government, utilizing both governmental and nongovernmental resources to plan for, respond to, and recover from an incident, regardless of cause, size, or complexity.

Incident Management Team (IMT): An Incident Commander and the appropriate Command and General Staff personnel assigned to an incident. The level of training and experience of the IMT members, coupled with the identified formal response requirements and responsibilities of the IMT, are factors in determining "type," or level, of IMT.

Incident Objectives: Statements of guidance and direction needed to select appropriate strategy(s) and the tactical direction of resources. Incident objectives are based on realistic expectations of what can be accomplished when all allocated resources have been effectively deployed. Incident objectives must be achievable and measurable, yet flexible enough to allow strategic and tactical alternatives.

Information Management: The collection, organization, and control over the structure, processing, and delivery of information from one or more sources and distribution to one or more audiences who have a stake in that information.

Initial Action: An action taken by those responders first to arrive at an incident site.

Initial Response: Resources initially committed to an incident.

Intelligence/Investigations: An organizational subset within ICS. Intelligence gathered within the Intelligence/Investigations function is information that either leads to the detection, prevention, apprehension, and prosecution of criminal activities—or the individual(s) involved—including terrorist incidents or information that leads to determination of the cause of a given incident (regardless of the source) such as public health events or fires with unknown origins. This is different from the normal operational and situational intelligence gathered and reported by the Planning Section.

Interoperability: Ability of systems, personnel, and equipment to provide and receive functionality, data, information and/or services to and from other systems, personnel, and equipment, between both public and private agencies, departments, and other organizations, in a manner enabling them to operate effectively together. Allows emergency management/response personnel and their affiliated organizations to communicate within and across agencies and jurisdictions via voice, data, or video-on- demand, in real time, when needed, and when authorized.

Job Aid: Checklist or other visual aid intended to ensure that specific steps of completing a task or assignment are accomplished.

Joint Information Center (JIC): A facility established to coordinate all incident-related public information activities. It is the central point of contact for all news media at the scene of the incident. Public information officials from all participating agencies should co-locate at the JIC.

Joint Information System (JIS): A structure that integrates incident information and public affairs into a cohesive organization designed to provide consistent, coordinated, accurate, accessible, timely, and complete information during crisis or incident operations. The mission of the JIS is to provide a structure and system for developing and delivering coordinated interagency messages; developing, recommending, and executing public information plans and strategies on behalf of the Incident Commander (IC); advising the IC concerning public affairs issues that could affect a response effort; and controlling rumors and inaccurate information that could undermine public confidence in the emergency response effort.

Jurisdiction: A range or sphere of authority. Public agencies have jurisdiction at an incident related to their legal responsibilities and authority. Jurisdictional authority at an incident can be political or geographical (e.g., city, county, tribal, State, or Federal boundary lines) or functional (e.g., law enforcement, public health).

Jurisdictional Agency: The agency having jurisdiction and responsibility for a specific geographical area, or a mandated function.

Key Resource: Any publicly or privately controlled resource essential to the minimal operations of the economy and government.

Letter of Expectation: See Delegation of Authority.

Liaison: A form of communication for establishing and maintaining mutual understanding and cooperation.

Liaison Officer (LNO): A member of the Command Staff responsible for coordinating with representatives from cooperating and assisting agencies or organizations.

Local Government: Public entities responsible for the security and welfare of a designated area as established by law. A county, municipality, city, town, township, local public authority, school district, special district, intrastate district, council of governments (regardless of whether the council of governments is incorporated as a nonprofit corporation under State law), regional or interstate government entity, or agency or instrumentality of a local government; an Indian tribe or authorized tribal entity, or in Alaska a Native Village or Alaska Regional Native Corporation; a rural community, unincorporated town or village, or other public entity. See Section 2 (10), Homeland Security Act of 2002, Pub. L. 107-296, 116 Stat. 2135 (2002).

Logistics: The process and procedure for providing resources and other services to support incident management.

Logistics Section: The Incident Command System Section responsible for providing facilities, services, and materials for the incident.

Management by Objectives: A management approach that involves a five-step process for achieving the incident goal. The Management by Objectives approach includes the following: establishing overarching incident objectives; developing strategies based on overarching incident objectives; developing and issuing assignments, plans, procedures, and protocols; establishing specific, measurable tactics or tasks for various incident management functional activities and directing efforts to attain them, in support of defined strategies; and documenting results to measure performance and facilitate corrective action.

Manager: Individual within an Incident Command System organizational unit who is assigned specific managerial responsibilities (e.g., Staging Area Manager or Camp Manager).

Metric: A measurable standard, useful in describing a resource's capability.

Mission Assignment: The mechanism used to support Federal operations in a Stafford Act major disaster or emergency declaration. It orders immediate, short-term emergency response assistance when an applicable State or local government is overwhelmed by the event and lacks the capability to perform, or contract for, the necessary work. See also Pre-Scripted Mission Assignment.

Mitigation: The capabilities necessary to reduce loss of life and property by lessening the impact of disasters. Mitigation capabilities include, but are not limited to, community-wide risk reduction projects; efforts to improve the resilience of critical infrastructure and key resource lifelines; risk reduction for specific vulnerabilities from natural hazards or acts of terrorism; and initiatives to reduce future risks after a disaster has occurred.

Mobilization: The process and procedures used by all organizations—Federal, State, tribal, and local— for activating, assembling, and transporting all resources that have been requested to respond to or support an incident.

Mobilization Guide: Reference document used by organizations outlining agreements, processes, and procedures used by all participating agencies/organizations for activating, assembling, and transporting resources.

Multiagency Coordination (MAC) Group: A group of administrators or executives, or their appointed representatives, who are typically authorized to commit agency resources and funds. A MAC Group can provide coordinated decision-making and resource allocation among cooperating agencies, and may establish the priorities among incidents, harmonize agency policies, and provide strategic guidance and direction to support incident management activities. MAC Groups may also be known as multiagency committees, emergency management committees, or as otherwise defined by the Multiagency Coordination System.

Multiagency Coordination Systems (MACS): A system that provides the architecture to support coordination for incident prioritization, critical resource allocation, communications systems integration, and information coordination. MACS assist agencies and organizations responding to an incident. The elements of a MACS include facilities, equipment, personnel, procedures, and communications. Two of the most commonly used elements are Emergency Operations Centers and MAC Groups.

Multijurisdictional Incident: An incident requiring action from multiple agencies that each have jurisdiction to manage certain aspects of an incident. In the Incident Command System, these incidents will be managed under a Unified Command.

Mutual Aid or Assistance Agreement: Written or oral agreement between and among agencies/organizations and/or jurisdictions that provides a mechanism to quickly obtain emergency assistance in the form of personnel, equipment, materials, and other associated services. The primary objective is to facilitate rapid, short-term deployment of emergency support prior to, during, and/or after an incident.

National: Of a nationwide character, including the Federal, State, tribal, and local aspects of governance and policy.

National Incident Management System (NIMS): A set of principles that provides a systematic, proactive approach guiding government agencies at all levels, nongovernmental organizations, and the private sector to work seamlessly to prevent, protect against, respond to, recover from, and mitigate the effects of incidents, regardless of cause, size, location, or complexity, in order to reduce the loss of life or property and harm to the environment.

National Response Framework (NRF): A guide to how the Nation conducts all-hazards response.

Nongovernmental Organization (NGO): An entity with an association that is based on interests of its members, individuals, or institutions. It is not created by a government, but it may work cooperatively with government. Such organizations serve a public purpose, not a private benefit. Examples of NGOs include faith-based charity organizations and the American Red Cross. NGOs, including voluntary and faith-based groups, provide relief services to sustain life, reduce physical and emotional distress, and promote the recovery of disaster victims. Often these groups provide specialized services that help individuals with disabilities. NGOs and voluntary organizations play a major role in assisting emergency managers before, during, and after an emergency.

Officer: The Incident Command System title for the person responsible for one of the Command Staff positions of Safety, Liaison, and Public Information.

Operational Period: The time scheduled for executing a given set of operation actions, as specified in the Incident Action Plan. Operational periods can be of various lengths, although usually they last 12 to 24 hours.

Operations Section: The Incident Command System Section responsible for all tactical incident operations and implementation of the Incident Action Plan. In ICS, the Operations Section normally includes subordinate Branches, Divisions, and/or Groups.

Organization: Any association or group of persons with like objectives. Examples include, but are not limited to, governmental departments and agencies, nongovernmental organizations, and the private sector.

Personal Responsibility: The obligation to be accountable for one's actions.

Personnel Accountability: The ability to account for the location and welfare of incident personnel. It is accomplished when supervisors ensure that Incident Command System principles and processes are functional and that personnel are working within established incident management guidelines.

Plain Language: Communication that can be understood by the intended audience and meets the purpose of the communicator. For the purposes of the National Incident Management System, plain language is designed to eliminate or limit the use of codes and acronyms, as appropriate, during incident response involving more than a single agency.

Planned Event: A scheduled nonemergency activity (e.g., sporting event, concert, parade, etc.).

Planning Meeting: A meeting held as needed before and throughout the duration of an incident to select specific strategies and tactics for incident control operations and for service and support planning. For larger incidents, the Planning Meeting is a major element in the development of the Incident Action Plan.

Planning Section: The Incident Command System Section responsible for the collection, evaluation, and dissemination of operational information related to the incident, and for the preparation and documentation of the Incident Action Plan. This Section also maintains information on the current and forecasted situation and on the status of resources assigned to the incident.

Pre-Positioned Resource: A resources moved to an area near the expected incident site in response to anticipated resource needs.

Preparedness: Actions taken to plan, organize, equip, train, and exercise to build and sustain the capabilities necessary to prevent, protect against, mitigate the effects of, respond to, and recover from those threats that pose the greatest risk. Within NIMS, preparedness focuses on the following elements: planning; procedures and protocols; training and exercises; personnel qualifications, licensure, and certification; and equipment certification.

Preparedness Organization: An organization that provides coordination for emergency management and incident response activities before a potential incident. These organizations range from groups of individuals to small committees to large standing organizations that represent a wide variety of committees, planning groups, and other organizations (e.g., Citizen Corps, Local Emergency Planning Committees, Critical Infrastructure Sector Coordinating Councils).

Prevention: The capabilities necessary to avoid, prevent, or stop a threatened or actual act of terrorism. Prevention capabilities include, but are not limited to, information sharing and warning; domestic counterterrorism; and preventing the acquisition or use of weapons of mass destruction (WMD). For purposes of the prevention framework called for in the PPD-8 directive, the term "prevention" refers to preventing imminent threats.

Private Sector: Organizations and individuals that are not part of any governmental structure. The private sector includes for-profit and not-for-profit organizations, formal and informal structures, commerce, and industry.

Protocol: A set of established guidelines for actions (which may be designated by individuals, teams, functions, or capabilities) under various specified conditions.

Public Information: Processes, procedures, and systems for communicating timely, accurate, accessible information on the incident's cause, size, and current situation; resources committed; and other matters of general interest to the public, responders, and additional stakeholders (both directly affected and indirectly affected).

Public Information Officer (PIO): A member of the Command Staff responsible for interfacing with the public and media and/or with other agencies with incident-related information requirements.

Publications Management: Subsystem that manages the development, publication control, publication supply, and distribution of National Incident Management System materials.

Reimbursement: A mechanism used to recoup funds expended for incident-specific activities.

Resource Management: A system for identifying available resources at all jurisdictional levels to enable timely, efficient, and unimpeded access to resources needed to prepare for, respond to, or recover from an incident. Resource management under the National Incident Management System includes mutual aid agreements and assistance agreements; the use of special Federal, State, tribal, and local teams; and resource mobilization protocols.

Resource Tracking: A standardized, integrated process conducted prior to, during, and after an incident by all emergency management/response personnel and their associated organizations.

Resources: Personnel and major items of equipment, supplies, and facilities available or potentially available for assignment to incident operations and for which status is maintained. Resources are described by kind and type and may be used in operational support or supervisory capacities at an incident or at an emergency operations center.

Response: The capabilities necessary to save lives, protect property and the environment, and meet basic human needs after an incident has occurred.

Retrograde: To return resources back to their original location.

Safety Officer: A member of the Command Staff responsible for monitoring incident operations and advising the Incident Commander on all matters relating to operational safety, including the health and safety of emergency responder personnel.

Section: The Incident Command System organizational level having responsibility for a major functional area of incident management (e.g., Operations, Planning, Logistics, Finance/Administration, and Intelligence/Investigations (if established)). The Section is organizationally situated between the Branch and the Incident Command.

Single Resource: An individual, a piece of equipment and its personnel complement, or a crew/team of individuals with an identified work supervisor that can be used on an incident.

Situation Report: Confirmed or verified information regarding the specific details relating to an incident.

Span of Control: The number of resources for which a supervisor is responsible, usually expressed as the ratio of supervisors to individuals. (Under the National Incident Management System, an appropriate span of control is between 1:3 and 1:7, with optimal being 1:5; or between 1:8 and 1:10 for many large-scale law enforcement operations.)

Staging Area: Temporary location for available resources. A Staging Area can be any location in which personnel, supplies, and equipment can be temporarily housed or parked while awaiting operational assignment.

Standard Operating Guidelines: A set of instructions having the force of a directive, covering those features of operations which lend themselves to a definite or standardized procedure without loss of effectiveness.

Standard Operating Procedure (SOP): A complete reference document or an operations manual that provides the purpose, authorities, duration, and details for the preferred method of performing a single function or a number of interrelated functions in a uniform manner.

State: When capitalized, refers to any State of the United States, the District of Columbia, the Commonwealth of Puerto Rico, the Virgin Islands, Guam, American Samoa, the Commonwealth of the Northern Mariana Islands, and any possession of the United States. See Section 2 (14), Homeland Security Act of 2002, Public Law 107-296, 116 Stat. 2135 (2002).

Status Report: Information specifically related to the status of resources (e.g., the availability or assignment of resources).

Strategy: The general plan or direction selected to accomplish incident objectives.

Strike Team: A set number of resources of the same kind and type that have an established minimum number of personnel, common communications, and a leader.

Supervisor: The Incident Command System title for an individual responsible for a Division or Group.

Supporting Agency: An agency that provides support and/or resource assistance to another agency. See Assisting Agency.

Supporting Technology: Any technology that may be used to support the National Incident Management System, such as orthophoto mapping, remote automatic weather stations, infrared technology, or communications.

System: Any combination of facilities, equipment, personnel, processes, procedures, and communications integrated for a specific purpose.

Tactics: The deployment and directing of resources on an incident to accomplish the objectives designated by strategy.

Task Force: Any combination of resources assembled to support a specific mission or operational need. All resource elements within a Task Force must have common communications and a designated leader.

Technical Assistance: Support provided to State, tribal, and local jurisdictions when they have the resources but lack the complete knowledge and skills needed to perform a required activity (such as mobile-home park design or hazardous material assessments).

Technical Specialist: Person with special skills that can be used anywhere within the Incident Command System organization. No minimum qualifications are prescribed, as technical specialists normally perform the same duties during an incident that they perform in their everyday jobs, and they are typically certified in their fields or professions.

Technology Standards: Conditions, guidelines, or characteristics that may be required to facilitate the interoperability and compatibility of major systems across jurisdictional, geographic, and functional lines.

Technology Support: Assistance that facilitates incident operations and sustains the research and development programs that underpin the long-term investment in the Nation's future incident management capabilities.

Terrorism: As defined in the Homeland Security Act of 2002, activity that involves an act that is dangerous to human life or potentially destructive of critical infrastructure or key resources; is a violation of the criminal laws of the United States or of any State or other subdivision of the United States; and appears to be intended to intimidate or coerce a civilian population, to influence the policy of a government by intimidation or coercion, or to affect the conduct of a government by mass destruction, assassination, or kidnapping.

Threat: Natural or manmade occurrence, individual, entity, or action that has or indicates the potential to harm life, information, operations, the environment, and/or property.

Tools: Those instruments and capabilities that allow for the professional performance of tasks, such as information systems, agreements, doctrine, capabilities, and legislative authorities.

Tracking and Reporting Resources: A standardized, integrated process conducted throughout the duration of an incident. This process provides incident managers with a clear picture of where resources are located; helps staff prepare to receive resources; protects the safety of personnel and security of supplies and equipment; and enables the coordination of movement of personnel, equipment, and supplies.

Tribal: Referring to any Indian tribe, band, nation, or other organized group or community, including any Alaskan Native Village as defined in or established pursuant to the Alaskan Native Claims Settlement Act (85 Stat. 688) [43 U.S.C.A. and 1601 et seq.], that is recognized as eligible for the special programs and services provided by the United States to Indians because of their status as Indians.

Type: An Incident Command System resource classification that refers to capability. Type 1 is generally considered to be more capable than Types 2, 3, or 4, respectively, because of size, power, capacity, or (in the case of Incident Management Teams) experience and qualifications.

Unified Approach: The integration of resource management, communications and information management, and command and management in order to form an effective system.

Unified Area Command: Version of command established when incidents under an Area Command are multijurisdictional. See Area Command.

Unified Command (UC): An Incident Command System application used when more than one agency has incident jurisdiction or when incidents cross political jurisdictions. Agencies work together through the designated members of the UC, often the senior persons from agencies and/or disciplines participating in the UC, to establish a common set of objectives and strategies and a single Incident Action Plan.

Unit: The organizational element with functional responsibility for a specific incident Planning, Logistics, or Finance/Administration activity.

Unit Leader: The individual in charge of managing Units within an Incident Command System (ICS) functional Section. The Unit can be staffed by a number of support personnel providing a wide range of services. Some of the support positions are pre-established within ICS (e.g., Base/Camp Manager), but many others will be assigned as technical specialists.

Unity of Command: An Incident Command System principle stating that each individual involved in incident operations will be assigned to only one supervisor.

Volunteer: For purposes of the National Incident Management System, any individual accepted to perform services by the lead agency (which has authority to accept volunteer services) when the individual performs services without promise, expectation, or receipt of compensation for services performed. See 16 U.S.C. 742f(c) and 29 CFR 553.101.

Made in the USA
Las Vegas, NV
10 August 2021